2006

To Bill
from Harold

A LIFE FOR EVERY SLEEPER

Japanese troops celebrate the fall of Singapore on 15 February 1942. Casualties among the defenders were: United Kingdom 38 496; Australian 18 490 including 1789 killed in action and 1306 wounded; Indian 67 340; local volunteer troops 14 382; a total of 138 708, of whom more than 130 000 became prisoners. Japanese casualties were 9824.
[127905]

A Life for Every Sleeper

A pictorial record of the Burma—Thailand railway

HUGH V. CLARKE

ALLEN & UNWIN
Sydney   London   Boston

First published in 1986
Second impression 1987
Allen & Unwin Australia Pty Ltd
8 Napier Street, North Sydney, NSW 2060, Australia
Allen & Unwin (New Zealand) Ltd,
60 Cambridge Terrace, Auckland, New Zealand

Allen & Unwin (Publishers) Ltd
Park Lane, Hemel Hempstead, Herts HP2 4TE, England

Allen & Unwin Inc.
8 Winchester Place, Winchester, Mass 01890, USA

National Library of Australia
Cataloguing-in-publication entry:

Clarke, Hugh V. (Hugh Vincent), 1919–   .
A life for every sleeper.

ISBN 0 04 909023 2.

1. Burma-Siam Railway—Pictorial works. 2. World War,
1939–1945—Prisoners and prisons, Japanese—
Pictorial works. 3. World War, 1939–1945—Conscript
labor—Pictorial works. I. Title.

940.54′72′520222

Library of Congress Catalog Card Number:

Set in 11.5/13 pt. Garamond by Setrite Typesetters Ltd, Hong Kong
Printed in Singapore by Singapore National Printers

Contents

Illustrations

Maps

Acknowledgements

This book is based on documents, photographs and maps preserved in the records of the Australian War Memorial and partly on my own experience as a member of 'D' Force in Thailand during 1943−44.

Many books have been written about the Burma−Thailand railway including my novel *The Tub*, published in 1962. These have been mostly subjective accounts by authors who were there. This book is an attempted objective summary of that great tragedy incorporating photographs which the War Memorial has acquired only recently. Some were taken by a Japanese surveyor during construction of the railway and donated to the War Memorial by Mr A.F. Seary, of Mareeba, Queensland, who was a former prisoner of war on the railway.

I am grateful for the generous assistance afforded me by the assistant director of the Australian War Memorial, Dr Michael McKernan, and members of his staff, particularly Ian Affleck for his assistance in the selection of the photographs. Another valuable source of information for this book has been A.J. Sweeting's account of the prisoner-of-war period in the official war history *The Japanese Thrust*. I am indebted to Richard Gilman of 'A' Force for his recollection of the dramatic joining of the two ends of the railway near Konkoita on 16 October 1943.

Like many former prisoners of war who worked on the railway I returned there (in 1978) and my impressions from that visit are recorded here briefly. The most recent development on the Burma−Thailand railway is a proposal, partly funded by the Australian government and involving the Snowy Mountains Engineering Corporation and the Australian−Thai Chamber of Commerce, to build a memorial to prisoners of war who died there. Snowy Mountains engineer Jim Appleby

A LIFE FOR EVERY SLEEPER

carried out preliminary work on the project in Thailand in 1985 and I am grateful to him for providing photographs for the final chapter of this book.

I would like to pay tribute to J.G. (Tom) Morris who initiated the move to establish the Hell Fire Pass cuttings at Konyu in Thailand as a permanent memorial. I am also indebted to my wife Patricia for her help and encouragement, and to my editor, Venetia Nelson.

Introduction

One of the most extraordinary engineering achievements of World War II was the construction of the Burma–Thailand railway. With unbelievably primitive tools for such a project and a total disregard for human life and suffering, the Japanese built a railway 415 kilometres long through one of the most rugged and pestilence-ridden areas in the world in the incredibly short span of twelve months. The cost was a life for every sleeper laid over its most difficult sections. Dead were 13 000 British, Australian, American and Dutch prisoners of war and an estimated 70 000 Asian civilian labourers. Australian dead numbered 2646.

The decision to build the railway was made by the Japanese Cabinet following the decisive defeat of its navy at the Battle of Midway in June 1942. At that time a large Japanese army was based in Burma and another in New Guinea and adjacent islands. Both depended for support and supplies on the navy which after Midway no longer enjoyed its former supremacy. The Japanese were aware that the British had surveyed a proposed railway linking Burma and Thailand in 1910 and that they had abandoned the project in 1912 because of the difficult terrain, endemic diseases and high monsoonal rainfall. To planners studying the map in Tokyo, however, the construction of a 415 kilometre railway seemed an obvious solution to supplying the army in Burma and thus avoid the hazardous sea route around Singapore and through the Straits of Malacca.

Accordingly two Japanese railway regiments totalling 12 000 men were assigned to the railway project—the 5th Regiment to be based at Thanbyuzayat in Burma and the 9th Regiment at Kanchanaburi in Thailand. The deadline for completion of the railway was August 1943 and in June 1942 the Japanese began moving Australian, British and Dutch prisoners of war to Burma and Thailand. The total workforce to be employed on the railway included some 51 000 British, Dutch

A LIFE FOR EVERY SLEEPER

and American prisoners of war, 9500 Australians and over 270 000 conscripted Asian labourers from China, Burma, Thailand, Malaya and Singapore.

Some experiences were common to all of the work forces sent to Burma and Thailand in 1942 and 1943, but as the forces were continually split up and spread along the route of the railway many experiences varied enormously from camp to camp. The first groups to arrive were composed mainly of fit men, while those which left Changi after April 1943 were made up of men in very poor physical condition and included large numbers of convalescents. At Changi prisoners of war had little contact with the Japanese and were subject to the discipline of their own officers. In Thailand they were suddenly thrown into direct and violent contact with Japanese engineers and Korean guards.

Prisoners put to work in base camps or in flat country coped reasonably well but those in remote camps in the mountains who worked on embankments, cuttings and bridges suffered unbelievable hardships. Until the coming of the monsoonal rain about the end of May 1943, living conditions were endurable. But as the incessant heavy rain turned bush tracks into impassable bogs and swelled the river until it became unnavigable prisoners of war in remote areas could not be adequately supplied. Their boots and clothes rotted away and they slowly starved while being literally worked to death. Malaria, dysentery and ulcers were ever present and with the monsoon came cholera.

A further factor for good or ill was the character of the individual Japanese camp commandants. Some were reasonable, a few compassionate but most were dedicated to one purpose—getting the railway through at any cost.

The first Australian prisoners of war to begin work on the railway were a group of 3000 men, known as 'A' Force, under Brigadier Varley. They had left Changi in May 1942 to work on airfields in southern Burma but in September 1942 were moved to Thanbyuzayat, the northern starting point of the line. Meanwhile, in late June 1942, a force of 600 British prisoners of war, under the command of Major R.S. Sykes RASC, had been moved to Bampong to begin preliminary work on the Thailand side and the following January 'Dunlop Force', of 900 Australians, under Colonel E.E. Dunlop, arrived from Java at Konyu on the River Kwai.

As batch after batch of British, Dutch, Australian and some American prisoners of war continued to converge on Thailand and Burma, the Japanese also began recruiting Tamils, Chinese, Malays and other civilian labourers from Burma, Singapore, Malaya, Java and Thailand. By October 1942 construction was under way but it is doubtful if the Tokyo planners or the Japanese engineers in Burma and Thailand had any conception of the magnitude of the task they were undertaking or the natural disasters that lay ahead.

The first official statement on the planned railway was made to prisoners of war at Thanbyuzayat on 15 September 1942 by Lieutenant Colonel Nagatomo, chief of the No. 3 Branch Office of Thai War Prisoners' Camp. It read:

It is a great pleasure to me to see you at this place as I am appointed Chief of War Prisoners Camp in obedience to the Imperial Command issued by His Majesty the Emperor.

The Great East Asiatic War has broken out due to the rising of the East Asiatic Nations whose hearts were burnt with the desire to live and preserve their nations on account of the intrusion of the British and Americans for the past many years.

There is therefore no other reason for Japan to drive out the anti-Axis powers of the arrogant and insolent British and Americans from East Asia in co-operation with our neighbours of China or other East Asiatic nations and to establish the Greater Asia Co-prosperity Sphere for the benefit of all human beings and to establish everlasting peace in the World.

During the past few centuries Nippon has made extreme endeavour and made sacrifices to become the leader of the East Asiatic Nations who were mercilessly and pitifully treated by the outside forces of the Americans and British, and Nippon without disgracing anybody has been doing her best up till now for fostering Nippon's real power.

You are all only the remaining skeletons after the invasion of East Asia for the past few centuries and are pitiful victims. It is not your fault but till your Governments wake up from the dreams and discontinue their resistance all of you will not be released. However I shall not treat you badly for the sake of humanity as you have no fighting power at all. His Majesty the Emperor has been deeply anxious about all War Prisoners and has ordered us to enable opening of War Prisoners Camps at almost all the places in the Southward Countries. The Imperial thoughts are inestimable and the Imperial favours are infinite and as such you should weep with gratitude at the Greatness of them and should correct or mend the misleading and improper anti-Japanese ideas.

I shall meet with you hereafter and at the beginning of the opening of the office I require you to observe the four following points:

I heard that you complain about the insufficiency of various items. Although there may be lack of materials, it is difficult to meet all your requirements.

A LIFE FOR EVERY SLEEPER

Just turn your eyes towards the present condition of the World. It is entirely different from pre-war times. In all countries and lands all materials are considerably short, and it is not easy to obtain even a small piece of cigarette or a small match stick, and the present position is such that it is not possible even for the needy women and children to get sufficient food.

Needless to say therefore that at such inconvenient place even our respectable Imperial Army is also not able to get mosquito nets, foodstuffs, medicines and cigarettes freely and frequently. As conditions are such, how can you expect me to treat you better than the Imperial Nippon Army. I do not persecute according to my own wish and it is not due to the expense but due to the shortness of materials at such distant places. In spite of my wishes to meet your requirements, I cannot do so with money. I shall however supply you if I can do so with my best efforts and I hope that you will rely upon me and render your lives before me.

I shall strictly manage all of you. Going out, coming back, meeting with friends, communications, possessions of money etc. of course shall be limited. Living manners, deportment, salutation and attitude shall be strict and according to the rules of the Nippon Army, because it is only possible to manage you all, who are merely rabbles, by the order of Military regulations. By this time I shall issue separate pamphlets of house-rules of War Prisoners and you are required to act strictly in accordance with these rules and you shall not at all infringe any of them by any means.

My biggest requirement from you is [no] escape. The rules for escape shall naturally be very severe. This rule may be quite useless and only binding to some of the War Prisoners, but it is most important for all of you in the management of the Camp. You should therefore be contented accordingly. If there is one foolish man who is trying to escape, he shall see big jungles towards the East which are absolutely impossible for communication, towards the West he shall see boundless Ocean and above all, in the main points of South and North, our Nippon Army is staying and guarding. You will easily understand the difficulty of complete escape. A few cases of ill-omened matters which happened in Singapore shall prove the above and you should not repeat such foolish things although it is a last chance after great embarrassment.

Hereafter I shall require all of you to work, as nobody is permitted to do nothing and eat as at present. In addition, the Imperial Nippons have great work to promote at the places newly occupied by them and this is an essential and important matter. At the time of such shortness of materials, your lives are preserved by the Military and all of you must reward them with your labour. By the hand of Nippon Army, railway works to connect Thailand and Burma have started to the great interest of the world. There are deep jungles where no man comes to clear them by cutting the trees. There are also countless difficulties and sufferings but you shall have the honour to join in this great work which was never done before and should do your best efforts. I shall check and investigate carefully about your non-attendance, so all of you except those who are really unable to work, shall be taken out for labour. At the same time I shall expect all of you to work earnestly and confidently every day.

In conclusion I say to you 'Work cheerfully' and from henceforth you shall be guided by this motto.

The above instructions have been given to you on the opening of the War Prisoners Camp at Thanbyuzayat.

Lt-Col Y. Nagatomo

When the exodus of prisoners of war from Changi to unknown destinations began in early 1942, no one had any knowledge of a proposed railway. Each departing force was denoted by a letter of the alphabet, beginning with 'A' Force 3000-strong, which left for Burma in May 1942. It was followed by 'B' Force, 1496-strong, which left Changi for Sandakan on the north-west coast of Borneo in July 1942. 'C' Force of 2200, including 563 Australians, embarked from Singapore for Japan at the end of November 1942. 'D' Force of 2780 British and 2200 Australians left Singapore on 14–18 March 1943 for Thailand and, although they did not know it at the time, they were headed for the railway. 'E' Force of 1000, including 500 Australians, followed by the end of March 1943, bound for Borneo.

The largest force, and next to depart from Changi was 'F' Force, 7000-strong including 3600 Australians. This group was railed to Thailand and marched to various jungle camps on the route of the proposed railway. 'G' Force was assembled by the Japanese as a reinforcement of 'E' Force but instead was sent to Japan in April 1943. It consisted of 1000 Dutch, 300 British and 200 Australians. 'H' Force of 3270, including 600 Australians, boarded trains for Thailand in May 1943. 'J' Force also left Changi in May, bound for Japan. Included in the party of 900 were 300 Australians, mainly convalescent.

Two smaller forces, 'K' and 'L', were purely medical parties. 'K' Force, consisting of 30 medical officers and 200 other medical ranks including five doctors and 50 others who were Australian, left Changi for the Burma–Thailand railway in June 1943. 'L' Force, made up of fifteen medical officers and 100 other ranks, left Changi for the railway in August 1943. A major role of 'K' and 'L' parties was to provide belated medical care for the army of civilians by then dying in thousands on the railway.

After the departure of all these groups the strength of Australians in Changi fell to less than 2500, few of whom were fit. Changi thus became a backwater until December 1943 when the remnants of 'F' and 'H' Forces began dribbling back from the completed railway.

1 Changi, Singapore, 26 January 1943. A ceremonial parade was held on Selarang Barrack Square to celebrate Australia Day. Members of 27 Infantry Brigade paraded under the command of Lieutenant Colonel C.H. Kappe. Shown above are members of 2/30 Infantry Battalion moving to flank to march past and members of 2/29 Infantry Battalion [43917]

2 One of the 50-metre attap huts used to accommodate up to 250 prisoners of war in Changi. Other prisoners were housed in the former British Selarang barracks built of brick and concrete. All of the accommodation was grossly overcrowded but was infinitely superior to that provided for prisoners of war sent to Burma, Thailand and elsewhere. [19189]

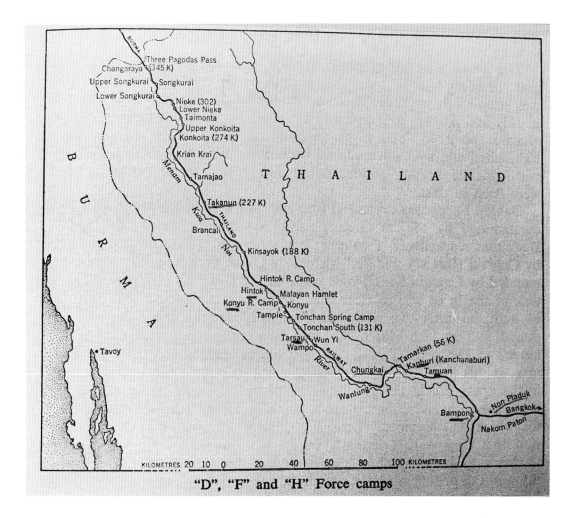

Map 1   The Burma–Thailand railway

'Work cheerfully . . .'

Lt-Col. Y. Nagatomo to 'A' Force, Thanbyuzayat, Burma, 1942

The 3000 men of 'A' Force sailed from Singapore on 15 May 1942 on two small, overcrowded, filthy steamers on which an epidemic of dysentery broke out almost immediately. After an unpleasant journey the two ships reached Victoria Point in southern Burma where 1017 men under Lieutenant Colonel C.E. Green disembarked. Three days later a further 1000 men, led by Lieutenant Colonel G.E. Ramsay, were unloaded at Mergui together with 500 British from Sumatra. The rest of the convoy went to Tavoy where they were joined by a Dutch party from Sumatra.

For the next few months the three parties, at their separate destinations, worked on airfield construction. After some initial misunderstandings the prisoners were treated fairly by the Japanese, who seemed unprepared for the large numbers being thrust into their care. Nevertheless the thought of escape was in the minds of many men and in June one of the first attempts at escape from Burma was made by eight Australians at Tavoy. All were members of the 4 Anti-Tank Regiment and were led by Warrant Officer Quittendon. They were soon recaptured and four days later were executed by a firing squad of sixteen guards. Their conduct to the end was exemplary. Brigadier Varley, who was compelled to witness the execution, recorded in his diary: 'The spirit of these eight Australians was wonderful. They spoke cheerio and good luck messages to one another and never showed any sign of fear. A truly courageous end.'

In August 1942 the parties at Mergui and Victoria Point were brought to Tavoy and work continued on that airfield until it was completed on 16 September. Later the movement of 'A' Force to start work on the railway began. Most of the prisoners were taken by ship to Moulmein and thence by cattle trucks to Thanbyuzayat.

The Japanese organised their work force into groups varying in size from 2000 to 12 000 men. In Burma two prisoner-of-war groups, Groups 3 and 5, operated, while in Thailand Groups 1, 2, 4 and 6 functioned, together with an additional 10 000 who came under Malayan prisoner-of-war administration ('F' and 'H' Forces) as distinct from the Thai administration. Thus by early October 1942, prisoners of war in Burma were spreading south from Thanbyuzayat clearing undergrowth, felling great trees and making embankments and cuttings. The equipment provided was primitive—picks, shovels and a hoe-like implement called a chunkel. Baskets and stretchers, made from bags and poles, were used to carry earth and rocks. In the beginning the Japanese fixed a work quota for earth-moving of 0.6 cubic metres per prisoner per day, but when they discovered the quota could be completed in half a day they gradually increased it until each prisoner was making the maximum effort. The same technique had been employed on the wharves in Singapore. In Thailand prisoner-of-war rock drillers started off drilling one metre a day but later were compelled to drill three metres a day. The average prisoner's maximum capability was cunningly gauged, then it was made the norm for all prisoners.

By November, prisoners in Group 3 were distributed in Burma between Thanbyuzayat and the 40-kilometre mark on the railway with conditions varying from camp to camp. One camp at Tanjin, at the 35 kilometre mark, was described by the official war history as

> the best experienced on the Burma section of the railway. The important factor in the treatment received by the prisoners was the character of the Japanese Camp Commandant . . . Lieutenant Yamada ranked as one of the best commanders that the force came under . . . In appearance rather grim and forbidding . . . he nevertheless exercised intelligence and tolerance in his camp administration. He rather stretched rules of the Imperial Japanese Army in regard to prisoners to ensure that Lieutenant Colonel Williams received treatment in accordance with his rank. When once he did complain that he himself was not being saluted as he moved about the camp it was as if to say: 'look here fellows after all I am the boss here; the least you could do is to pay a little respect occasionally.'

Events took a turn for the worse with the arrival of 200 Korean guards to take over guard duty at camps in Burma. Treated as an inferior race by the Japanese they took out their resentment and frustrations on the prisoners and were to earn an unequalled reputation for brutality and viciousness in both Burma and Thailand as the railway progressed.

In December the Japanese reaffirmed their uncompromising attitude to escape attempts by executing an Australian and three Dutchmen. In spite of this drastic deterrent the following February three Australians made a determined attempt to reach India. They were Major A. Mull, Sapper A. Bell and Gunner K. Dickinson. A few miles north of Moulmein, Dickinson fell out exhausted and was recaptured, taken back to Thanbyuzayat and shot. The other two had travelled a further 160 kilometres when they ran into a pro-Japanese native patrol. In the ensuing encounter Mull was killed and Bell badly wounded. On being returned to Thanbyuzayat Bell was also shot.

By March the prisoner-of-war work force in Burma was spread between Thanbyuzayat and Meiloe at the 75 kilometre camp. At this stage there were some 9534 prisoners under the command of Brigadier Varley, including 4465 Australians, 481 British, 194 Americans and 4394 Dutch. An additional group of 1850 prisoners not under Varley's command also worked in the area. The bulk of the Australians were based at Meiloe. A British-American force was laying rails towards the Kun Knit Kway and the Dutch were concentrated around camps at the 45 and 70 kilometre marks.

As the mobile rail-laying force advanced, work on cuttings, embankments, roads and bridges became more exacting; the Japanese engineers were determined that nothing would delay the rapid progress of the line.

A relic of the 75 kilometre camp was presented to the Australian War Memorial after the war by one of its former prisoner-of-war inmates, Private J.E. Fraser of the 2/4th Machine Gun Battalion. This was the original Japanese construction plan for the area. In the following extract from his covering letter, Mr Fraser explains how he got it and a consequence of his theft:

> The plan you have is the original which the Japanese issued. It represents the whole of the foundation for the Railway Line in Burma. It commenced at a town known as Thanbyuzayat (which is 43 miles south of Moulmein), extends approximately 113 kilometres and terminates at the border of Thailand.
>
> You may observe the alteration of figures on the plan cease just past 75 kilo.
>
> It was at this stage the plan came into my possession. We were camped at a place known as 75 Kilo camp. I noticed several Jap oficers intensely interested in a paper. After their dispersal, I watched one Jap officer place the plan in a leather case, and hang it in his hut. After he had gone out I went and put my hand through the window and took the plan out of interest, not knowing at the time what it represented.

The next day an announcement was made to the effect that any Japanese papers found were to be returned immediately. Knowing the consequences I decided to keep the plan.

The loss of this plan caused hindrance to the extent that we dug a 30 metre cutting which later proved to be a 30 metre embankment...

In April 1943 there was an influx of native labour onto the line following the enlistment of Burmese youths by the Japanese for either labour or defence. About this time the wet season began, earlier than expected, and by May 1943 the string of camps extending south-west from Thanbyuzayat were wallowing in seas of mud. Day and night the rain poured down from leaden skies, drenching miserable shelters and rotting clothing and boots. Cholera broke out, first among the wretched Asian labourers and then among the prisoners.

By June the forward camps were at the 105 and 108 kilometre marks and the Japanese engineers were under increasing pressure from higher authority to get the line finished regardless of cost. As Brigadier Varley noted at the time, they 'will carry out schedule and do not mind if the line is dotted with crosses'. In the forward jungle camps, men were now working up to 24-hour shifts and there were no holidays. As well as cholera, malaria, dysentery and tropical ulcers added to the abject misery of men who were mostly without boots or uniforms. This lack of protective clothing was one of the chief causes of skin injuries, which led to vicious tropical ulcers. Australian, British and Dutch doctors worked incredibly long hours with ingeniously improvised surgical instruments and drugs and disinfectants manufactured from whatever substance they could get their hands on.

Meanwhile the base camp at Thanbyuzayat was being bombed by Allied bombers from India. On 12 June 1943 nine men, including five Australians, were killed and eight wounded. In another raid three days later seventeen men were killed including thirteen Australians. Many others were wounded. As the year went on 'A' Force camps stretched south beyond the Three Pagoda Pass into Thailand and by September 1943 the mobile line-laying force had reached the 108 kilometre mark. From there the Japanese ordered that prisoners of Group 3 were to lay the rails as far as the 150 kilometre mark where they would meet parties working from the Thailand end. Disease-ridden prisoners now began working shifts of 24 hours on and 24 hours off as the Japanese drove to keep the work on schedule.

3 Thanbyuzayat railway station, the Burma terminal of the railway, is 72 kilometres south of Moulmein. Prisoners of war in 'A' Force began work on the railway at Thanbyuzayat in September 1942 and by the following March were spread over a 75 kilometre stretch of track. At this stage some 9534 prisoners including 4465 Australians, 481 British, 194 Americans and 4394 Dutch were at work in the area. In April 1943 the line was heavily reinforced with Asian labourers. [P406/40/38]

4, 5 Building an embankment at Ronsi in Burma. The earth was dug and carried in baskets and in bags slung from a pole carried by two men. Ant-like processions of prisoners moved hundreds of tons of earth in this fashion. The railway was a rosary of cuttings, bridges and embankments—all back-breaking tasks. [P400/40/32 and P406/40/29]

"THE BAG AND POLE"
METHOD OF CARRYING DIRT AND STONE
John D. Korsch

6 Mergui, Burma, May 1942. Australian prisoners of war carrying ballast for road-building. They are using the bag-and-pole method which was used widely in building embankments on the railway. Drawing made by Corporal J.D. Korsch while a prisoner of war. [34440]

7 Bridge-building at Ronsi, 25 kilometres from Thanbyuzayat. One of the most hazardous operations on the railway was bridge construction. Apart from the limited use of elephants the only equipment available was manpower, and fatal accidents occurred almost daily. [P406/40/35]

8 Line-laying at Ronsi with 70 kilometres to go to reach the Burma–Thailand border. A British-American force was engaged in this work and followed closely on those engaged in clearing jungle, building embankments and cutting through hills and mountains. [P406/40/34]

9 Prisoners of war grinding rice for 'pap' which was watery boiled rice usually served for breakfast. Lunch consisted mainly of firmer boiled rice while dinner was generally a cup of boiled rice and a watery vegetable soup. [157876]

10 Australian prisoners of war carrying sleepers in Burma, 70 kilometres from the Thailand border. Any kind of mechanical equipment was rarely seen on the railway. The entire project was carried out by manpower, dynamite and primitive tools. [P406/40/26]

11 Prisoners of war and Asian civilian workers building a bridge in Burma. Over 15 kilometres of bridges were built over the entire railway and some 30 000 trees were cut down to provide timber for girders. Primitive methods of pile driving were used, the power being provided by prisoners repeatedly raising the pile driver with ropes and letting it drop. By early 1945 such bridges became targets for Allied bombing. [118879]

12 Prisoners of war working on cookhouse duties. The most prized job in any prisoner-of-war camp was in the cookhouse. Not only were cooks and cooks' offsiders spared the labour and bashings on the railway but they had access to more food and rest. [P406/40/12]

13 Construction of a bridge at Konkoita, which was the joining point of the lines extending north from Bampong in Thailand and south from Thanbyuzayat in Burma. Prisoners dreaded the prospect of having to work on these crazy structures, falls from which were usually fatal. [P406/40/2]

14 Prisoners of war moving on to another camp after completing their section of line. In the early stages of construction they moved on foot, often over distances of up to 100 kilometres. As the line neared completion they were privileged to travel by train. The author worked in six different camps over a period of twelve months. [P406/40/11]

15 Bridge-building at Ronsi in Burma. Over 15 kilometres of bridging was constructed within the total 415 kilometres of railway. To the disbelief of the prisoners who built them, trains eventually travelled over them until Allied bombers began to destroy them systematically. [P406/40/33]

16, 17 Australian prisoners of war putting down sleepers and laying lines. This work was done quickly over flat country, but there was little of that in Burma and Thailand. When the lines were laid to a bridge or cutting, pressure on the prisoners always intensified. The Japanese engineers then began 'speedo' tactics, bashings proliferated, and men were overworked mercilessly up to 18 hours at a stretch. [P406/40/27 and 28]

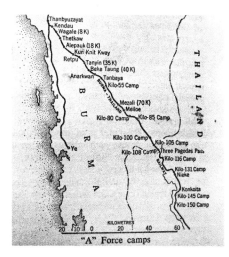

"A" Force camps

Map 2   'A' Force

18   A trainload of sleepers in Burma. For the thousands of prisoners of war spread along the route of the railway the arrival of sleepers meant the approaching end of their particular task and the prospect of a move to something better. All too often they moved to disaster areas—a cutting holding up the line or a behind-schedule bridge. [P406/40/25]

19 The headquarters of the Japanese 5th railway regiment of the Southern Army Railway Corps at Kanchanaburi. The other Japanese regiment, the 9th, also responsible for construction of the railway, was based at Thanbyuzayat in Burma. Kanchanaburi was linked by rail to Bampong on the Bangkok−Singapore railway by March 1943. When 'F' Force disembarked at Bampong in April 1943, however, the prisoners were forced to walk some 300 kilometres to its final destination. [P406/40/40]

'A special savagery . . .'

2

Dunlop Force, Thailand

In the Thailand sector where Dunlop and succeeding forces were to be employed the track of the line ran over level country to Kanchanaburi and Tamarkan, the site of two bridges, one concrete and one of wood. From there the line followed the left bank of the Kwai Noi River into thick jungle and massive clumps of bamboo. Approaching Wampo the route led into hilly country and beyond Tarsau into rugged mountains covered with dense jungle and extensive clumps of bamboo. The conquest of this kind of country called for the construction of improvised viaducts and bridges and massive earthworks and rock cuttings. The lifeline of the project was the river and the commander of 'D' Force, which followed Dunlop Force, Lieutenant Colonel C.A. McEachern, described its role:

> The river Kwai Noi was of great importance during the construction of the railway. In the dry season, although full of shoals and rapids, it is navigable for barges towed by motor launches up to Takanoon and in the rainy season as far as Krekonta. The river was used as a transport system for water supply and for washing; it was also thick with fish, though P.O.W. were rarely able to avail themselves of this. Occasionally the Japanese exploded dynamite charges below water and obtained some quantity of fish (about 70 lbs) and at Chunkai a turtle was landed, both with improvised rods and lines.
>
> The jungle was full of every kind of biting insect both by day and night, a great number of snakes were killed but only a few cases of snake bite were reported (one fortunately a Japanese). Both at 248 Camp and at Chunkai audiences at a concert round a camp fire, were dispersed by a big snake being attracted to the fire—or the music!

On one occasion a herd of some hundred wild pigs crossed the river below 211 camp where P.O.W. were working. Many were killed with spades and pickaxes etc. and eaten.

The jungle throughout was full of exotic orchids, beautiful butterflies and lizards. A large variety of birds were seen and heard. The scenery often was magnificent.

The work in this sector was very varied, consisting of jungle clearing, tree felling, rock cutting, bridge and viaduct building, besides embankment and cuttings, many of great depth. Often the rock was so close to the surface that great difficulty was found and extra heavy work caused in finding sufficient soil for embankments. The rock generally was hard, jagged limestone like petrified sponge, which wore out boots in a few days and cut hands and feet.

Dunlop Force consisted of 878 Australians under the command of Lieutenant Colonel E.E. Dunlop AAMC. They departed from Java for Singapore on 4 January 1943 and from Singapore by train on 20 January, arriving at Bampong four days later. From Bampong they went on to the Konyu area where there were some 3000 British troops already showing signs of complete breakdown from semi-starvation, disease and overwork. Here a group of some 600 Dutch prisoners also came under Dunlop's command and after two weeks of sleeping in the open the whole force moved to Hintok Road camp over three kilometres from the river.

In an interim report on experiences of POW working camps Colonel Dunlop described the work in the Hintok area and the attitudes of the Japanese Army engineers and guards as follows:

The Hintok section of the line was technically most difficult being extremely rocky, involving big embankments and cuttings. The main working camp was sited so that the men had to march to work over rough hills up to 3 to 4 miles night and morning. They frequently left in darkness in the morning, 0700/0800 I.J.A. time, the march and the day's work sometimes keeping them out up to 16 hours a day. During the worst blitz of the railway drive, there was no day of rest for over 3 months. Work consisted largely of hand drilling with crude drills, rock clearing after dynamite, hauling logs in the jungle, bridge building and scratching earth from amongst the stones which was carried in baskets to build embankments. In the rock cuttings in particular the heat and glare at times, were well nigh unendurable and the rocks hot enough to blister the feet of bootless men. In general a worse enemy was the incessant downpour of the Monsoon Rain . . .

The administration of working camps was divided between local I.J.A. Camp Commander and Staff with many Korean Guards and the I.J.A. Engineer personnel who took charge of workmen to direct their activity daily. On the whole the Camp Commander and Staff shared in the responsibility for the hopelessly inadequate camp and medical arrangements for P.O.W.s. In my experience, however, most of the brutality and actual violence meted to our prisoners was by the engineers. In the Konyu—Hintok area the engineer company was commanded by Lt Hirota. This officer on occasion personally ordered sick out of hospital and his presence on the line was associated with waves of brutality. He personally, on occasion, threw stones at prisoners and felled them with sticks. At his command on occasion exhausted men who fell out of working parties were beaten and maltreated. On one occasion a Sgt who was ordered out of hospital and manhandled for some hours died the next day. Blows and kicks and sadistic punishments were a routine measure. On occasion men with diarrhoea and dysentery were not permitted to leave their work. A special savagery was often shown to sick men. The Medical N.C.O. Cpl, later Sgt Okada, was a willing tool in the hands of the Engineers and on one occasion of a General's inspection and after days of argument about reduction of Hospital sick figures, undertook to reduce these figures by marching some 50 men into a hiding place in the jungle. Although the men were obviously very ill with large tropical ulcers, protem odema etc. they were then handed over to the Engineers to roll 60 gallon oil drums over a rough hill track for several kilos to a compressor site. These are examples of routine daily brutality. A particularly obnoxious feature was the intentional employment of men with appalling inflamed and swollen feet for log hauling in the jungle and rock clearing. There were naturally exceptions to this bad behaviour, certain overseers behaving more reasonably.

At the end of March 1943 the first of 'D' Force had begun to arrive in the area and part of it brought the strength of Hintok camp to about 1000.

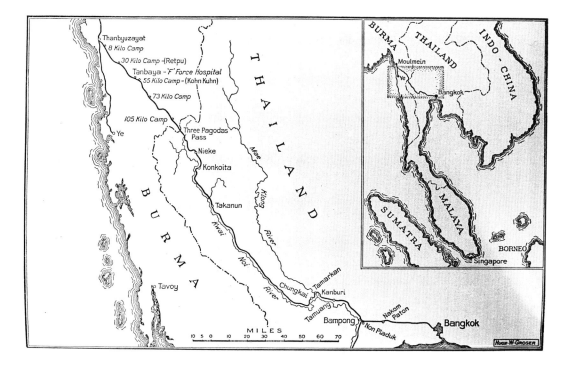

Map 3   'D', 'F' and 'H' Force camps

The cutting and the pack of cards bridge

3

'D' Force, Thailand

'D' Force consisted of 2780 British and 2220 Australians under the command of Lieutenant Colonel McEachern and began moving from Singapore to Thailand in mid-March 1943. The Australians were organised into three battalions, 'S', 'T', and 'U' and dispersed between Kanchanaburi and Hintok. Colonel McEachern with part of 'S' battalion moved to Hintok and took over administrative duties from Colonel Dunlop, leaving him free to concentrate on the overwhelming medical problems then besetting the prisoners on the line.

I was a member of 'T' battalion of 'D' Force. The journey from Singapore took between four and five days during which we travelled jammed into enclosed steel trucks with no ventilation or facilities and limited to one pint of water a day. At Bampong we were searched and transferred to flat-top rail trucks which carried us over a newly laid line to Kanchanaburi which was as far as the line reached at that time.

We climbed off the train and spread out in the surrounding scrub and to our surprise our guards packed up and went. Other Japanese in the area showed no interest in us so we began trading with the Thais, erecting shelters and cooking eggs and other food obtained from the locals. For nearly a week we lived a life of comparative freedom and plenty and some men were convinced that the Japanese had released us to fend for ourselves because of the food shortage in Singapore. That belief was shattered when a group of aggressive, shouting guards arrived one morning and herded us together. From them we learned that our brief freedom had been the result of a mistake. The Singapore guards had been ordered to deliver us to Kanchanaburi and they had obeyed their orders to the letter. The fact that other guards, intended to take delivery of us, had not turned up was no concern of theirs. The new guards, who were mainly Koreans, herded us on to trucks which took us away from civilisation through giant clumps of bamboo into the hills to the base camp of Tarsau. There we met indescribably gaunt British and Dutch prisoners, some with blood from dysentery running down their legs and most mottled with filthy sores. My greatest shock was the sight of beri-beri victims carrying their melon-sized testicles before them.

We spent the night at Tarsau and marched sixteen kilometres south in the morning to begin work on the railway. After erecting tents in a stony creek bed near its junction with the river we began building a low embankment. The Japanese engineer in charge of the job set reasonable tasks and discouraged his 200 men from bashing us. The job entailed digging and blasting out clumps of bamboo and carrying earth in baskets and improvised stretchers. The work was completed in two weeks and we marched further south to an old established camp at Wampo where a massive embankment was being built but running a long way behind schedule. The British occupants of the camp were in an even more diseased and dejected condition than those we had seen at Tarsau. Immediately we were divided into two shifts, day and night, and as part of the day shift I was soon at work. My first sight of the embankment put me in mind of the pyramids. Towering over 30 metres above us it had been built up by men with baskets and bag stretchers. We were told it had to be completed within two weeks, by which time the line-laying gang was due at Wampo. We worked in parties of six—two men digging at the base of the embankment with pick and shovel and the other four with two rice-bag stretchers carrying the dirt up the steep incline.

As the deadline drew closer the tempo of work increased and bashings and torture became part of the Japanese 'speedo' effort. The final shift lasted 30 hours and as the embankment neared completion men were dropping unconscious in their tracks. When we marched north we left behind 100 men.

Our new destination was Konyu, two and a half days' walk from Wampo. On Anzac Day, 25 April 1943, we halted in a small clearing in the jungle-covered plateau and were informed that this was our new camp—when we built it. It was to be known as Konyu 3.

The job site was at the end of a 500 metre track under a canopy of towering bamboo and was to be a cutting through a great rocky spur. Far below, beyond a sea of bamboo, the river wound north like a silver ribbon. The cutting, which was to become known as 'Hell Fire Pass', consisted of one section about 500 metres long by eight metres high linked to another about 80 metres long and over 26 metres high. Our tools were picks and shovels and dynamite.

We began work in teams of two with hand drills and eight-pound hammers.

Initially we were ordered to drill two metres in the rock after which we were permitted to return to camp. The strongest men were able to complete this task by about four pm, and accordingly the Japanese raised the daily quota to three metres 'finish go home'. This soon taxed the waning strength of the big men and for others it was well-nigh impossible in spite of bashings and other tortures. Usually the Japanese blasted twice during each shift and as soon as the echoes of each dynamite explosion rolled away teams of men moved in to clear away the shattered rock while the drillers made more holes for the next blast.

Here there were no holidays and work proceeded at a frenzied pace day and night. Some elephants arrived on the job to haul logs but their Burmese drivers soon died of cholera, and about the same time the monsoon came, bringing with it that fearsome disease on a scale which was to cut an enormous swath through the workforce.

The incessant rain churned every camp along the line into a muddy swamp and in the all-pervading wet, tents, boots and clothing disintegrated rapidly. The cutting began to take shape and our original work party of 400 dwindled as cholera, dysentery, cerebral malaria and bashings filled shallow, sodden graves beside the camp. A party of some 200 British officers augmented our group but they too soon thinned out under the vicious attentions of Itchi Noi, a Japanese engineer said to be a de-ranked officer.

As the rails approached the cutting in June an air compressor arrived together with a group of Japanese jackhammer operators. The radiator of the compressor leaked and for several weeks my job was to carry cans of water all day from the creek to keep the radiator from boiling dry. Eventually I was replaced by an elephant which carried bamboo containers of water from the creek as a full-time task. To maintain the ever-shrinking work force more British and Australian prisoners arrived including 'U' battalion of 'D' Force under Captain Reg Newton and a group of newly arrived 'H' Force. The men of 'H' Force, mostly unfit to begin with, camped about 200 metres along the muddy track from the main Konyu 3 camp and before long they were dying in dozens from cholera, bashings, starvation and exhaustion.

My job at this stage was drilling by hammer and tap. This involved working in pairs, one man wielding the hammer while the other kept rotating the drill in the hole. I would start with a 25 centimetre drill and, as the hole became deeper, change to a longer drill, using finally a metre-long drill which was the depth required for blasting. Drilling was made easier if water was poured regularly into the hole and it was also necessary to keep removing dirt and crushed rock from the hole by means of a long piece of thick-gauge wire flattened at one end like a spoon. These pieces of wire were favoured by some Japanese engineers as instruments for flogging tardy workers. Twice each shift the holes were plugged with dynamite and the fuses lit by prisoners with cigarettes provided by the engineers. After the blast another group of prisoners would move in to remove the rock and dirt while the drilling of more holes began.

The length of each shift increased until the shifts overlapped, with most men working up to eighteen hours a day.

About this time I was given a job as NCO in charge of some twenty 'light men'. Our task was to start about midday cutting bamboo up to four inches in diameter and 40 feet high and dragging it down to the cutting. At about dusk we gulped our meagre meal of rice and returned to the cutting to light fires to provide illumination for the night shift. In addition to the bamboo fires there were small carbide lamps and if any of these lamps was allowed to go out the man responsible and the NCO in charge was bashed. Extra lighting was provided by bamboo containers filled with dieseline and hessian wicks. Keeping the cutting brightly lit was a constant backbreaking job and the only moments of peace came when the darkness imperceptibly merged into dawn and far below the mist-covered river would materialise, letting us know that the shift was coming to an end.

As the cutting grew deeper and longer the engineers brought in miniature railway lines and a set of iron skips to speed up disposal of the blasted rock. These half-dozen metal barrows with railway wheels were loaded with rock and tipped over the side to help form an embankment. This innovation provided entertainment for some of the Japanese engineers who ordered them loaded to overflowing and then insisted that each be manned by two prisoners standing on the brake rods while others pushed at great speed. Inevitably the trucks gained such momentum that the prisoners on the brake rods were unable to jump off before the trucks hurtled over the embankment. Not only did these games result in hideous injuries to some of the victims but the task of retrieving the trucks and wheels and reassembling them provided backbreaking exercise for other prisoners.

The commander of 'D' Force, Brigadier C.A. McEachern, had this to say about the attitude of the Japanese to prisoners of war working on the railway:

During 1943–43 the average Japanese claimed to know nothing of the Hague or Geneva Conventions. Those who admitted to some knowledge of International Law and these conventions expressed what can be taken as the Japanese Army attitude that a signature to the Hague Convention by Japan was only binding on the Government and not on the Army. They took the view that it was dishonourable to be taken as a prisoner and that, therefore, P.O.W. had no rights or status and were slaves of the

Emperor for life. We must be punished for fighting against Japan and made to correct our anti-Japanese ideas.

In view of this it is not surprising that the Japanese authorities in charge of P.O.W. failed to observe even the more important provisions of International Conventions respecting P.O.W.

When it was pointed out to the Japanese Garrison Comd. at Mergui that if he permitted two men who had attempted to escape, to be shot, he would be committing a breach of International Law, he indicated that only the Japanese Army regulations were binding in the Japanese Army.

The Japanese did not consider human life of any value when viewed in the light that the railway must be pushed on regardless of cost. This attitude was openly professed by Japanese camp commandants who have frequently stated that 'even if men die they should do so gladly as they are working for the Emperor and the Railway must go on.'

Discipline was enforced by brutality. For example when standing to attention in front of a Jap soldier should the P.O.W.'s heels be 1″ apart he would be severely beaten. Bashings and other forms of punishment for minor offences were common.

The Japanese camp staffs and guards held a totally erroneous conception of their personal powers, authority and status in relation to P.O.W. No attempt was ever made by the Japanese to correct the impression that they could do as they wished with P.O.W.

Further, the system of enforcing discipline was to make the P.O.W. Commander of each camp responsible for much of the administration and discipline of P.O.W., while at the same time denying him the facilities essential to such control.

In some cases the Korean guards were kept down by the Japanese and the treatment they received was reflected on P.O.W. against whom they were encouraged to be brutal. In other cases they were given full authority when they were even worse. At times a soldier would be placed in charge of a party and his word on all matters was final. If a protest was entered against an order or act the reply was 'you must obey all the orders of the I.J.A.'

Frequently two Japs would be placed in charge of the same task, when each would insist on it being carried out according to his own personal ideas. This resulted in the P.O.W. performing the task to receive beatings from both Japs. Despite repeated protests this difficulty was never overcome.

Dual control was much in evidence as between guards and railway

A LIFE FOR EVERY SLEEPER

engineers. It was quite evident that there was no co-operation between them, each being jealous of his own rights. The engineers would say that the P.O.W. would continue working for another two hours; because the guard had not been consulted he would in all probability order them to cease work, and at times engineers and guards came to blows over these matters.

While the cutting took its continuing toll of prisoners another ambitious engineering project was under construction between Konyu and Hintok with labour supplied from Hintok camp. This was a bridge 400 metres long and 27 metres high built of green timber and other jungle material. It was known as the 'Pack of Cards' bridge because it fell down three times during construction. Victims of this particular project included 31 men killed in falls to the rocks below and 29 beaten to death on the job.

By the time I was evacuated from Konyu with malaria, ulcers, dysentery and suspected appendicitis in July only some 50-odd men of the original 'T' battalion remained. The Hintok–Konyu sector was finished by mid-September, but well before then the Japanese had begun sending large numbers of sick by barge down-river to the hospital camp at Tarsau. The mortality of 'D' Force was eighteen per cent, but among its component battalions it ranged between 12 and 50 per cent.

20   Closed steel rice trucks in which prisoners were transported from Changi to
Thailand. There were 36 men to a truck and the journey took five days. Men and their
gear were so tightly packed that sleep was possible only in shifts. By day the prisoners
stifled in the overheated steel trucks and by night they froze. Toilet facilities were
non-existent apart from occasional stops and food consisted of two small rice meals a day.
A Japanese guard travelled in each truck and occupied a position near the partly closed
sliding door which was the only source of ventilation. [157866]

21 The main road from Thailand to Burma. During the monsoon period this road was the only line of communication and thousands of prisoners of war trudged through the mud to various camps along its route. A common sight before the railway was completed was also the passage of hardy young Japanese troops on their way to the Burma front. [128452]

22 Prisoners of war marching north through Konyu. Most movement along the narrow track was at night and Australians at K3 camp often saw former friends trudging by with groups of 'F' Force heading for even worse camps further north. They also watched in silence as groups of young Japanese troops moved north dragging small mountain guns and other equipment. [P406/40/06]

23 A barge transporting sick prisoners of war and stores on the River Kwai in Thailand. Barges were an important form of transport during the construction of the railway but during the monsoon months which started at the end of May the river rose so high and flowed so fast that operation of barges ceased. Because of this upriver camps were unable to receive vital food supplies. [128451]

24 Barges moored on the bank of the Kwai Noi river. The river was navigable as far as Takanun in the dry season and as far as Konkoita in the wet and was of great importance both as a means of transport and for its water supply. It was also rich in fish, which prisoners were seldom permitted to catch. [P406/40/08]

25 A diesel rail-car passing over one of the longest trestle bridges constructed on the Burma–Thailand railway on 21 October 1945. The bridges and embankment near Wampo were built in March–April 1943 and were completed in a frenzied burst of 'speedo' or non-stop work. Prisoners of war returning south over this part of the line usually lit up cigarettes, if they had them, until this section was safely negotiated. [122323]

26 The cutting at Konyu known as 'Hell Fire Pass'. Over 500 yards long and up to 80 feet high, it claimed the lives of many prisoners of war. Work on the cutting began on 25 April 1943 when men of 'T' battalion of 'D' Force were halted at the site and half of them put to work building a camp in virgin bamboo jungle while the other half began the gargantuan task of making the cutting with hand drills, picks and shovels, baskets and dynamite. Rail-laying parties reached the cutting in June 1943 and more prisoners, including the fittest of 'O' and 'P' battalions, Newton's 'U' battalion of 'D' Force, a battalion of 'H' Force and some British prisoners, arrived. Hours of work lengthened to 18 hours a day and this continued for about six weeks until the cutting was completed. While it was being made 68 men were beaten to death. [157859]

27, 28 The cholera block and kitchen at Konyu. These two photographs of Konyu 3 Camp Thailand were copied from a set of photographs I bought in Melbourne in December 1945. From my inquiries they originated from material used in the Rabaul War Crimes trials. I have been unable to discover who took the photographs but as an original member of 'T' battalion of 'D' force which occupied Konyu 3 I can vouch for their authenticity. They were obviously taken during the monsoon period when the cholera tents were first erected. How the photographer, who must have been one of the artillerymen who made up 'T' battalion, took and developed the photographs is beyond belief—let alone how he got them to Rabaul.

29 A northbound train passing over a trestle bridge near Kensoyak on the Burma–Thailand railway. Building such bridges from jungle material was one of the most dangerous tasks allotted to prisoners of war. One such bridge near Hintok was named the 'Pack of Cards Bridge'. Built of green timber, fastened with wooden wedges, spikes, bamboo ties and cane rope, it was 400 yards long and 80 feet high. It fell down three times during construction and in that time 31 men were killed in falls and 29 beaten to death. [122309]

30 The interior of a typical 180 metre attap-roofed hut. The attap was transported to various camps along the River Kwai and bamboo supports were cut from the local jungle. The whole structure was held together by ties stripped from the bark of certain trees. Sleeping space for each man was about two and a half feet in width. Housing for prisoners in some of the smaller camps like Konyu 3 consisted merely of rows of hastily erected rotting tent flies. [157878]

31 Transporting attap on the River Kwai. A kind of thatching, attap was used along the length of the railway to roof the huts in prisoner-of-war camps. It was rainproof but a harbour for bugs and lice which were a continual torment to the prisoners. It was also a popular hiding place for diaries and other prohibited items. [P406/40/13]

32 Elephants were used extensively in Burma and Thailand during construction of the railway. Their main task was to haul logs from the jungle. At Konyu Australians were astonished to find themselves sharing the same narrow muddy track with six of these lumbering animals. When the Burmese drivers died of cholera the elephants refused to perform heavy tasks which were taken over by the prisoners of war. These six elephants bathed in a small creek upstream of Konyu camp so that by the time water reached the prisoners of war it often resembled a thick soup. [P406/40/09]

33 Prisoners of war driving dog spikes at Takanun. North of Takanun three great cuttings were made and many ravines had to be bridged. Gradients were often very steep and the laying of the lines brought an end to the terrible toils of the preceding months. [P406/40/20]

34 A 'U' battalion mess parade at a camp in Thailand during the building of the railway. Following the outbreak of cholera one of the precautions insisted upon by the medical officers was that each man had to sterilise his eating utensils in boiling water before receiving his rice. River water was boiled in kerosene tins before each meal. At this stage, about mid-1943, very few prisoners had boots; some of the more resourceful made footwear from wood or old tyres. [128455]

The long march

4

'F' Force, Thailand

'F' Force, consisting of 3600 Australians and 3400 British under the command of Lieutenant Colonel S.W. Harris of the 18th British Division, began leaving Changi on 16 April 1943. Thirteen trains were required to move the force to Thailand under conditions similar to those endured by previous forces. Many of the men in the force were unfit to begin with but the Japanese organisers at Changi assured them that they were going to a place where food was more plentiful and the climate more congenial.

Disembarking at Bampong, each trainload of prisoners faced a march lasting over two weeks over a distance of some 300 kilometres covered in fifteen stages of about twenty kilometres each. Lieutenant Colonel S.W. Harris described the march in a history of 'F' Force preserved in the Australian War Memorial:

> Marching was invariably done by night, between 2000 hrs and 0800 hrs. Except for the first two stages the road was merely a rough jungle track, capable of taking wheeled traffic in dry weather only. Long stretches of it were corduroyed, which, with snags and holes, made marching in the dark difficult and dangerous. Falls, resulting in sprains and even broken legs, were frequent. Control on the march was virtually impossible as all torches had been confiscated during a military search at Bampong. At the same time, the fate of stragglers was uncertain, as Thais armed with knives hung on the tail of the column in certain areas, ready to strip off the equipment of any man who fell behind. It is probable that some at least of the 20 men still missing from the force met their end at the hands of these bandits.

Daily thunderstorms started on 30 April and the monsoon proper broke just after the earlier parties reached their destination. The later parties thus had to contend with even worse marching conditions. The road surface became slippery and treacherous and long stretches were flooded and even totally washed away. The night march now frequently lasted for 14 or 15 hours instead of 12, and during the day's rest exhausted men had nowhere to shelter from the rain except on sodden ground under trees and bushes. It was unfortunately the less fit British parties which had to contend with these worsened conditions and this undoubtedly accentuated their already inferior physical state on reaching final camps.

Even trained infantry in good condition would have found a march of this length and in these conditions an arduous one. But this force included men of all services and of every known physical category except A.1, for even those rated fit among them had for more than a year subsisted on an inadequate diet, with consequent weakness from malnutrition. In addition there were the 2000 and more unfit, included in the force as a result of the orders of the I.J.A. Hundreds of these were convalescents whose sole reason for being there was that the I.J.A. had guaranteed them a journey by rail and motor-transport to a comfortable camp where rest and good rations were assured. Among them were men suffering beri-beri, post diphtheric hearts and other ailments, which rendered their survival impossible from the moment they were sent marching from Bampong. These unfit men, the number of whom steadily increased, proved from the first a great strain on the fit, who had to help and even carry them from camp to camp. In addition, every party was burdened with as many small (3 and 6 gallon) containers and as much medical gear as it could carry. Thus, even those who were fit at the start of the march were seriously exhausted or themselves unfit at the end of it.

The staging camps were jungle clearings at the side of the road, at about 20 kilometres distance from each other, generally (but not always) near water. Accommodation consisted of a cookhouse and open-trench latrines, and flies abounded: but of shelter there was none, except in two of the fifteen camps where tents were available for about one hundred men only. These camps were under the command of junior N.C.O.s of some I.J.A. movement control organisation, apparently unconnected with either the Malaya or Thailand P.O.W. Administration. These men, whose behaviour was often harsh and unreasonable, evidently had orders to push the marching columns forward as fast as possible, and the greatest difficulty was experienced everywhere in obtaining permission to leave behind even the worst of the sick.

Food, which consisted of rice and vegetable stew, was supplied in insufficient quantities to maintain the strength of men engaged on such a march, and water was often short. At Kamburi staging camp drinking water had to be bought by the prisoners from a privately owned well.

Lieut-Col. Harris tried to get this put right, but the abuse was not stopped until after the last party of 'F' Force had passed through. When 'H' Force arrived, however, some weeks later free water had become available there.

From Kamburi Col. Harris sent back a letter to Lieut. Fukuda pointing out that a tragedy was in the making. This letter detailed the immediate steps necessary to avert disaster.

It was difficult for the men to obtain sufficient rest during the day-time halts at these staging camps; for, apart from the lack of shelter, parties were often required to carry water or perform fatigues for the Japanese. This could have been avoided if the I.J.A. had detached permanent fatigue parties of sufficient size at each staging camp to close up on the force when the march was completed. Such parties could also have done much to improve the sanitation of the staging camps, all of which had previously been used by coolie gangs and which became progressively worse day by day.

The strain fell particularly heavily on the Medical Officers and orderlies, as they had to attend to casualties on the line of march and hold sick parades during the day's halt, not only for their own sick but also for the steadily increasing numbers left behind by previous parties. Also at every camp the day ended and the march began with an argument with the Japanese N.C.O. as to the number of sick men to be left. The end of this was always that seriously sick men, with blistered and ulcerated feet, and such illnesses as dysentery, beri-beri and malaria, were driven out of the camp to join the marching party, often with blows.

At Tarso the staging camp was of the usual type, but in the vicinity was the headquarters of both the I.J.A. Railway Engineers and the Thailand P.O.W. Administration, with a permanent P.O.W. camp and hospital, besides an I.J.A. hospital. When Advance H.Q. reached this staging camp (which, far from being the base camp of the force, proved to be at only one-third of the distance to destination) Col Harris visited the H.Q. of the Thailand P.O.W. Administration; but his reception there was so unfavourable and indeed offensive that it was evident a breach existed between the two administrations, presumably owing to jealousy at Malaya's retention of control over 'F' Force during its stay in Thailand. There was ample confirmation later that this jealousy existed, and to it can be attributed some of the misfortunes of the force.

The proximity of the hospitals at Tarso gave rise to hopes that Force H.Q. would be able to secure proper attention and accommodation there for the more seriously ill. On the night of our arrival it was necessary to restrain the I.J.A Corporal in charge of the staging camp from striking with a stick the sick men whom he had arbitrarily decided to send on the march. From the A.I.F. party which arrived the following morning Major Wild took 50 sick men for inspection by the I.J.A. Medical Officer at Tarso, who told the Corporal that 36 of them were quite unfit to march that night. Later, a written order that these men should not be made to march was obtained from the Japanese M.O. and was conveyed by his Sgt-Major to the Corporal: but he chose to ignore it. The same evening the 36 men were paraded and the Corporal ordered all but 10 of them to march. When Major Wild and Major Hunt, AAMC, remonstrated, they were beaten with bamboos in front of the men, and a bone in Major Hunt's hand was broken. Finally 17 of those sick were forced on the road. Of these, 3 were carried back after covering a few hundred yards, and the remainder were as usual helped or carried by their comrades to the next staging camp. Among the latter was the Rev. Ross-Dean of the A.I.F., who died at the next camp shortly afterwards.

Similar scenes were being enacted daily at every staging camp along the road. Hundreds of unfit were being rendered seriously ill by this treatment, and the whole force was being rapidly infected with malaria, dysentery and diarrhoea. In addition, the health and physique of the fit men also was deteriorating under the strain, so that they also were rendered more liable to infection.

Finally, at Konkoita staging camp, after a fortnight's marching, every party was quartered in immediate proximity to hundreds of coolies, who were suffering from some intestinal disease, of which numbers died daily. The whole area was heavily fouled and infested with a plague of flies. The I.J.A. pretended that the deaths were due to dysentery; it soon became certain that it was, in fact, cholera. Konkoita was the focal point of the infection which caused cholera to break out a few days later at all of the working camps to which the force was dispersed.

At Konkoita 700 A.I.F. of Parties Nos. 1 and 2, under Lieut-Col. S.A.F. Pond, OBE, 2/29 Bn A.I.F. (Lieut-Col. Kappe, Comd A.I.F. Contingent was also in the camp but hoped to move forward), were halted and placed under the command of Lieut. Maruyama of the I.J.A. Engineers. This party of 700 was subsequently detached from the I.J.A. Administration of 'F' Force and for all practical purposes came under the control of the Engineers until they rejoined the force at Nieke in December. Lieut-Col. Banno, the I.J.A. Commander of 'F' Force, made his first appearance at Tarso on 8 May in a lorry with the British officers of the Rear H.Q. On 9 May he took on Col. Harris with them, leaving the remaining three officers of Adv. Force H.Q. to follow on when the last party left Tarso. Two stages beyond Tarso Col. Banno suddenly ordered all the officers of the Rear H.Q. to dismount from the lorry with the medical stores which they were carrying to start a wayside hospital for the marching troops, while he proceeded up the road another 150 kilos to Nieke with Col. Harris. This incredible action had serious results, as the services of Lieut-Col. Huston were thus denied to the force during the first critical six weeks, together with the consignment of medical stores, which could not be brought up later by road owing to the breakdown of the road in the monsoon and were not brought up even by river.

Col. Banno arrived at Shimo-Nieke on 10 May by lorry, Col. Harris being the only P.O.W. with him. This was to be the H.Q. Camp. It consisted of two partially roofed huts and seven large unroofed huts in a partly cleared hollow in the jungle. There was a small natural stream to provide water for all purposes. The camp had previously been occupied by coolie labour.

During the next few days some I.J.A. stores arrived from Bampong and a small hut was roofed for Col. Banno and his office. The roofed huts were occupied by I.J.A. guards.

No shelter whatever was supplied for Ps.O.W.—not even for a hospital, an M.I. Room or a cookhouse.

The first batch of troops arrived on 13 May (Party 3 and remains of Parties 1 and 2) and thereafter continued to arrive daily.

Thunderstorms by this time were a daily and nightly occurrence until the monsoon proper broke in Shimo-Nieke on 17 May and spread slowly northwards. From then until well into September rain was incessant and heavy day and night. It was a rarity for more than four hours to pass without rain. There was one break of 24 hours in June and another in July.

The Force Comd protested to Col. Banno against the circumstances of the march and the lack of roofs. No satisfactory reply was received. The most obvious necessity was for a hospital for the sick as they arrived. It was already clear that the force would arrive heavily infected with malaria, dysentery, diarrhoea and septic sores on feet and legs.

Col. Banno explained that only the H.Q. would remain at Shimo-Nieke. The remainder of the force (excluding the 700 A.I.F. left at Konkoita, which was to be known as No. 4 Camp) would be distributed to other camps.

By the end of May 'F' Force was distributed as follows:

No 1 Camp	Lower Sonkrai	about 1800 Australians
No 2 Camp	Sonkrai	1600 British
No 3 Camp	Upper Sonkrai	393 Australians
No 4 Camp	Konkoita	700 Australians
No 5 Camp	Changaraya	700 British

The headquarters camp and base hospital with a staff of some 300 was located at lower Nieke and some 550 Australians and 800 British had yet to arrive in the work area.

By the end of June under the incessant downpour of the monsoon the Japanese engineers were demanding a maximum effort from the prisoners regardless of their state of health. The work was heavy and the hours long, seven days a week, on projects such as clearing jungle, building bridges and roads, hauling logs, digging cuttings and building embankments. The section of the railway was completed about mid-September and for the first time since May a holiday was granted.

Of the 3662 Australians in 'F' Force, 1060 died up to May 1944 and of a similar number of British 2036 died. Of these cholera claimed 637.

Infamous conditions and cholera

5

'H' Force, Thailand

As progress on the railway fell further behind schedule the Japanese demanded more men, and accordingly 'H' Force was raised in Singapore in April 1943. It consisted of 3270 British, Dutch, American and Australian prisoners under the command of Lieutenant Colonel Humphries with Lieutenant Colonel Oakes as second in command. The 600 Australians in the force were under the command of Lieutenant Colonel Oakes. Like 'F' Force it was to remain under the administrative command of the Japanese Army authorities in Malaya and to suffer from jealousies between the Malayan and Thai administrations.

The force travelled by rail to Bampong in May 1943 under circumstances similar to those which preceded it and from there the men walked to various destinations between Tonchan and Hintok, the headquarters of the force being established at Tampie. On arrival each group had to clear the jungle and erect makeshift camps and in no instance was there sufficient cover to shelter the men allocated to each area. All fit men and large numbers of sick were immediately pressed in to work on the railway, leaving only the extremely sick to dig latrines, erect cookhouses, bury the dead, chop wood and generally maintain the basic requirements of a camp.

The Australians in 'H' Force set out from Bampong on 13 May on a 90-mile walk to Tarsau, arriving six days later. On 21 May they reached Konyu 2, later known as Malayan Hamlet where they were to assist men of 'D' Force already working on the massive cutting. No preparations had been made for their arrival so their first task was to clear the jungle and build a camp. A few days later the exhausted men were put to work in up to 15-hour shifts of 200, one to work by day and the other by night.

By June sickness, bashings and exhaustion had reduced the strength of working shifts from 200 to 150 men and on the 16th of that month the first case of cholera was reported. On that date also 266 British prisoners arrived to join Oakes' force. Within nine days 72 men had died from the disease. The medical officer, Major Kevin Fagan, who with the padre Father Marsden, had rendered outstanding service to the sick on the long march, now faced impossible odds as cholera raged through the camp. Major Fagan and his medical orderlies worked almost non-stop with over 450 patients in the so-called hospital.

By the end of June only 120 men were fit to work and the camp was overrun by lice and rats. Conditions were similar in the other five 'H' Force camps spread along twenty miles of jungle, each camp being sited for its convenience to the railway rather than for considerations of health, water and general suitability. Food consisted mainly of boiled, poor-quality rice and a seaweed-like vegetable. By 22 August 1943 Oakes' force had 217 dead, including 106 Australians, and 100 'fit' men were moved north to Konkoita for further railway work.

One of the 'H' Force parties, numbering 320, consisted almost entirely of officers who had been promised before they left Changi that they would be engaged in administrative duties when they reached Thailand. Many of them were either elderly or unfit or both. On arrival at Tonchan south they were put to work on the railway. In spite of their protests they were compelled to work with Asian labourers and degraded in every possible way. During the cholera epidemic they had to bury dead and dying Asian labourers and were employed as porters carrying equipment and rations over distances of six kilometres.

In a report on general conditions Lieutenant Colonel Humphries, commander of 'H' Force, wrote:

> Hospital accommodation in the camps consisted throughout of primitive improvisations of split bamboo, inner fabric of tents etc. The Japanese, whilst acknowledging the necessity for hospital facilities, did nothing to assist in the provision of same, and the conditions under which these soldiers suffered through the various stages of their diseases, and under which many of them unfortunately died, are indescribable in a report of this nature. They can best be described as filthy charnel houses, and but for the untiring efforts of the Medical Officers and orderlies, the death toll, heavy as it was, must have been doubled or even trebled. Japanese guards were heard to say that they hoped the sick would die and thus save Japanese rice. Medical stores were practically nil—palm leaves having to be used for bandages.

I cannot recollect a single instance of the Japanese Administration providing anything, except one or two native kwalies, in the nature of a cookhouse or domestic utensil. Every bit of cooking, disinfection, food distribution, water storage, ablution etc. etc., was carried out by jealously guarded and laboriously portered utensils of our own provision or improvisation. No lighting was ever provided, even surgical operations were performed in the open by moonlight or the light of a camp fire. The hours of work continued long—so much so that the majority of the men never saw their camp by daylight. It was the monsoon season and it rained almost incessantly. No facilities existed, and no opportunities were given, for drying of clothes, cleansing of bodies, or resting, and it is not surprising that with this combination of infamous conditions, disease should be rampant. Malaria, dysentery, beri-beri, and above all, what the I.J.A. resourcefully ordered to be described as 'Post Dysenteric Inanition' on death certificates, but which was actually starvation—already stalked through the Camps of the Force. Then, without warning, Cholera epidemics swept down amongst us. Immediate representations for the cessation of movement were spurned and in point of fact, owing to the depletion of the labour force by death, movement became increasingly frequent and larger in character. The result was inevitable. The disease spread and notwithstanding the noble efforts of our own Medical personnel, every camp throughout the Force was quickly affected. The death rate was heavy, and many stories of inhumanity could be told of our captors during this period if time and space permitted in this report. It is perhaps sufficient to say at this juncture, that 880 out of 3270 people, representing some 27%, lost their lives. Figures which need no further comment and which add to the unanswerable indictment of the Japanese administration, inefficiency, and callousness.

Conscript Asian labour

6

'K' and 'L' Forces, Thailand and Burma

In addition to the prisoner-of-war work force of some 61 000 the Japanese at the end of 1942 resorted to many ruses to recruit an additional labour pool of over 270 000 civilian labourers. They included Chinese, Burmese, Thais, Indians, Malays and Eurasians. As prisoners of war began moving north the Japanese placed advertisements in Malayan newspapers seeking labourers for work periods of up to three months in Thailand. Free rail travel, housing, food and medical services were offered together with pay at the rate of one dollar a day. The response was negligible so the Japanese resorted to press-gang methods. Free picture shows were advertised at various theatres around Malaya and when full the doors were locked and all males in the audiences put aboard trains and railed to Thailand. Later, as all civilians had to register to receive their rice rations, the Japanese were able to assess the male population and began demanding 50 to 70 per cent of males in villages for their labour force. Many young men evaded this by taking to the jungle and remaining in hiding.

As pressure for completion of the railway built up it became increasingly difficult for the Japanese to replace people dying in Thailand. Java was then exploited with even more attractive rates of pay promised as well as advances of up to 100 dollars for the three-month contract. Similar methods were used in Burma. Needless to say three-month contracts proved valueless as no labourers returned to their homes during the first eighteen months. Once they reached Thailand and Burma they found themselves herded into unhygienic half-built camps with no medical facilities, inadequate rations and yoked to a relentless grind in which nothing mattered but completion of the railway.

In 1943 by the time the monsoon season had set in in Burma and Thailand, a series of decaying camps stretched between Thanbyuzayat in Burma to Kanchana-buri in Thailand. A steady deluge of rain poured down on the sodden jungle and the earth became a vast impassable sea of mud. Flimsy shelters housing prisoners of war and Asian labourers rotted away, as did their clothing and boots, and out of the mire emerged the most fearsome spectre of all—cholera. It attacked prisoners of war and civilian labourers alike, but the civilians lacked the discipline and hygiene of POW camps and they had no doctors. All along the route of the railway they died in hundreds. Some were buried in mass graves but others just wandered into the jungle and their bodies became continuing sources of infection.

By June 1943 yet another hazard was becoming commonplace, in the shape of Allied bombers bent on destroying supply dumps and bridges along the line.

It is doubtful if any of the Army planners in Tokyo could have foreseen the gruesome results of their policies and as far as the Japanese engineers were concerned their orders were to push the railway through regardless of cost. But by June 1943 the cost was becoming apparent, particularly among the civilians. Japanese authorities in Changi suddenly issued orders for the formation of a medical party consisting of 30 doctors and 200 medical orderlies. Five of the doctors and 50 others were Australians and the whole party was known as 'K' Force. A second medical party, 'L' Force, was formed of fifteen doctors and 100 other ranks. The role of both these parties was to provide belated medical care for survivors of the army of civilians then working and dying on the railway.

On arrival in Thailand all officers of 'K' Force were marched to Japanese Medical Headquarters where they were received by Colonel Hayakawa, commander of the Sanitary Corps. He delivered an impressive speech to the effect that all great engineering achievements of the world had been carried out in the face of tremendous medical problems. He described how the filthy white Yankee had built the trans-American railway with Chinese and Japanese coolie labour, thousands of whom had died. He ended his address by saying that before he could allow the doctors to start work he had to be sure that they had sufficient knowledge. Accordingly they would all have to sit for a two-hour examination. Anyone who failed would be put to work as a coolie. The questions were:

1. Number, name, rank, age, date and place of qualification, any specialist qualifications, where captured and how that place was arrived at from home country, what route was followed and what ports were called at en route.

2. The British Army was having a lot of trouble with malaria in Assam. What methods of prophylaxis were adopted by the British Army?

3. How much water was allowed to British front-line troops during active engagements, what methods of water sterilisation were used in the British Army?

4. The signs, symptoms, diagnosis and treatment of cholera. Describe the cholera virus, what were the best methods of culture and identification?

After the examination the officers were ordered to return next day for their results. When they returned to Medical Headquarters a Japanese major said he had great pleasure in informing them that all had passed with honours. The force was then dispersed among Asian labour camps along the railway where disease in all forms was rife, particularly cholera, dysentery, malaria and tropical ulcers. The average civilian camp at this time was a tumble-down conglomeration of shelters in a sea of mud, excreta and food refuse. Attached in ones and twos to civilian camps the men of 'K' Force embarked on a soul-destroying period of improvisation and daily toil from dawn to beyond dark. In spite of their dedication the Asian labourers continued to die in hundreds.

As time went on a situation developed reminiscent of the fuzzie wuzzie angels of the Kokoda Trail. It was found that in the majority of camps the Asian labourers looked after the men of 'K' Force. They were appreciative of any efforts made to help the sick and showed great generosity with gifts of food and items from their piteously few possessions. Through their kindness the majority of 'K' Force escaped the more extreme forms of vitamin deficiency.

35, 36 Asian workers recruited in Malaya, Java, Thailand and Burma travelling to work camps on the railway. Conditions for many of these workers were worse than those under which prisoners of war worked. When they reached Thailand they were herded into unhygenic half-built camps with no medical facilities and inadequate rations. Lacking the organisation and discipline of the prisoners of war they died in thousands. The Australian official war history *The Japanese Thrust* estimates the civilian death toll at between 70 000 and 90 000. [122301, 122303]

37 Asian workers on the railway at Wampo siding, Thailand, in October 1945. No one knows just how many civilian labourers died on the railway but the official history of the 2/19 Battalion records that of the 270 000 Asians impressed to work on the line only some 30 000 were ever traced or repatriated after the Japanese surrender. [122300]

38 Asian workers on the roof of a Burma-bound train in Thailand. Building the railway was a horrifying experience for most of the slaves employed on it. After its completion travelling on parts of it could be equally terrifying. On one long viaduct the speed limit was five kilometres an hour and derailments along the length of the line were frequent. Originally planned to transport 3000 tons daily, the target reached was about 1000 tons. [122328]

39 Montard women loading gasoline at Thanbyuzayat. In April 1943 the young people of Burma were being enlisted by the Japanese into either the 'Blood Army' or the Sweat Army—to defend or work for their country. [P406/40/37]

40 Asian labourers working on a bridge at Sonkrai or Ronsi. These unfortunate civilians lacked the medical officers who saved so many POW lives. They also lacked the discipline and sanitation essential to preserve life in such circumstances. [P406/40/22]

41 Asian labourers carrying sleepers at Takanun. The man on the left appears to be wearing a rice sack and has an ulcerated foot. Ulcers on the feet and legs were common among prisoners of war also and led to many amputations. [P406/40/18]

The Burma and Thailand lines join!   7

In early October 1943 the line from Thailand and the line from Burma were rapidly approaching each other. On 13 October in Burma after a short spell while several collapsed cuttings ahead were being repaired, the line-laying party, reinforced by 300 Dutch prisoners of war, resumed laying rails at a frantic pace. At one stage they worked 33 hours straight and, on 16 October 1943, the line joined at Konkoita, at about the 145 kilometre mark, with the line from Thailand.

Gunner Richard Gilman, 2/10 Field Regiment, a member of 'A' Force, recalls the dramatic occasion:

> There were signs of consternation and doubts among the Japanese engineers as the time for the joining of the railway lines being pushed forward from Burma and Thailand drew nearer. It was rumoured that in departing from the original British survey the Japanese had taken a number of short cuts and miscalculated to the extent that the lines approaching from the two directions instead of meeting would, if not redirected in good time, pass one another leaving a gap of some hundred of yards between them. It was never really established that such a catastrophe was likely to occur, but it was noted by prisoners on both sides of the railway that the Japanese engineers seemed to be ordering some sudden changes in the direction of the embankments and the lines over the last several kilometres of their course prior to their joining near the Three Pagoda Pass.
>
> As the day for the joining of the lines came closer there was an air of expectancy and excitement among the Japanese and the prisoners alike.

For the Japanese engineers and guards it signalled the completion of a momentous undertaking and a sense of fulfilment of a mission which would bring them merit in the eyes of the Emperor and the acclaim of their countrymen as well as advancing the strategy of their High Command for an assault on India mounted from Burma with equipment and troops moved across the railway from Thailand.

For the prisoners it spelt disbelief that a project which they had often thought impossible could have been achieved and utmost relief that their travail was almost over. In recent months a time limit and target date had been imposed by the High Command in a bid to complete the rail link before the more extreme monsoon conditions made the task more difficult and to accelerate plans for an offensive into India from northern Burma. The engineers and guards had responded to the 'speedo' order with fanatical zeal, intensified by their fear of dire consequences and loss of face should they fail to complete the task on schedule. For the prisoners, that 'speedo' had involved more brutality from the harassed and short-tempered guards and engineers, and more insistence by the Japanese camp commanders that quotas on the work parties would be maintained no matter how weak and disabled were those individuals who were declared by the Australian Camp medical officers to be unfit for work.

For the men actually laying the sleepers and rails as they came up on railway bogies over the completed line from the supply base in Burma, the pressure became almost intolerable as the time for the joining of the lines came closer. The onset of the monsoon rains was intensifying and the line-laying prisoners toiled interminably in mud and slush on the newly built embankments. Having walked through heavy rain some ten kilometres from their camp to the railhead the prisoners would wait sometimes for hours until new supplies of sleepers or rails came forward. As these supplies were irregular and unreliable the men would sometimes be kept on the job for shifts from twenty-four to thirty hours with their only nourishment a plate or two of rice carried out to them from the camp by their no more fortunate fellow prisoners. Lacking sleep, and weakened for want of food and by the heavy work of manhandling sleepers and railway lines which were pinned to the sleepers by dog spikes driven in by heavy sledge hammers, the prisoners toiled in a dazed, almost unconscious state. Oblivious to the mud under their feet and the driving rain the men would be utterly exhausted as they waited for the next supply of sleepers and with the already laid and dog spiked rails pillowing their heads. With the rain falling steadily on their upturned faces they would fall into a heavy sleep having posted one of their number, in rotation, as a lookout to warn them of the approach of the next consignment of sleepers and rails lest the wheels of the railway bogies sever a row of heads. Release from these nightmare conditions was eagerly contemplated.

Except for the nationalities involved and the costumes being worn, the scene on the day of the joining of the line resembled a western movie in the Hollywood tradition. There was the same air of expectancy as the two teams of line layers approached one another from the two directions; the clanking of hammers upon metal as dog spikes were driven into the sleepers; the puffing locomotives coming up to the railheads from both directions; the shouting and posturing of the dignitaries responsible for the successful completion of the railway. The Japanese senior officers looked awkward and self-conscious in their small caps and over-large jackboots. A military band played airs which seemed not a little off-key to the prisoners with their western-type musical orientation. Of necessity almost, there had to be a film to record the event for propaganda purposes both at home in Japan and in the Japanese-occupied countries in east and south-east Asia within what the Japanese Government described as the 'Greater East Asia Co-prosperity Sphere'. The producers and directors of the film were scurrying about looking important and, at the same time, embarrassed and self-conscious in their too new looking military uniforms which, as civilians, they had probably been obliged to wear in this military zone.

The film makers' plan was to use the prisoners in a line-laying scene to fit the last and joining section of rail into place and to drive home the dog spikes pinning the rail to the sleeper. When the time came to select the bit-players for this scene, the film men viewed the gaunt, skinny and near-naked prisoners with evident horror. How could these bony and under-nourished specimens as they stood barefooted and clad only in G-strings or lap-laps, be depicted on film as fit and contented men happy to be a part of the all-conquering Japanese Army and be working for the glory of the Emperor? The answer was found in part by the property department which provided 'costumes' for the several dozen prisoners who were hand-picked for the final line-laying scene. These men were fitted out with Japanese shirts, shorts and black sandshoes. These film stars, as they were immediately dubbed by their comrades suffered a good deal of ribald chaffing as they were called 'pansies' or even less complimentary names.

The cameras rolled, the band played a suitably triumphant air, and the selected prisoners—having been once rehearsed—performed their last line-laying rite. They carried the rail on their shoulders to the final remaining gap in the line, dropped it to the ground with a resounding bang, manhandled it into position on the sleepers, and drove home the dog spikes with a practised skill.

As the last spike was ready to be driven a most important but self-conscious looking senior and overweight officer of the Japanese Army came forward and was presented with a heavy sledge hammer to perform the symbolic driving of the last spike. Panting with the weight of the hammer this portly dignitary aimed a feeble blow at the head of the spike which he missed completely and gave the rail a resounding clang instead. Bracing himself and looking quite dismayed at his own clumsiness, the officer took a much shorter grip of the hammer and managed to drive the spike a fraction into the sleeper to be finished off by a lithe engineer who leaped to his assistance.

For the prisoners the whole episode of the joining of the lines near the Three Pagoda Pass was both farcical and pathetic. While they could not but smile at the antics of the Japanese as they enacted the final scene with so many Hollywood trimmings, their thoughts were on the futility of the 'achievement' and upon the tragic and unnecessary deaths of so many of their comrades.

For the prisoners, the line-laying ceremony had one remaining element of fun. Those of their number who had been selected and suitably costumed to take part in the final scene were prone to rejoice and swank their new shirts, shorts and footwear. Ironically, they were not even allowed to retain these small offerings as payment for their services. To the accompaniment of cheers and jeers from their mates the 'film stars' were deprived of their bounty by an unsmiling Japanese quartermaster and his staff who walked down the line of dandified prisoners collecting their uniforms in large bags and leaving the men standing bare and exposed-looking in their G-strings.

The ceremony was capped for the Japanese engineers and guards by a celebration dinner in which, judging from the sounds of revelry, generous portions of saki were served. For the prisoners there was little but anti-climax following the ceremony. They did however receive an extra ration of rice, which they were glad enough to have.

Of the 11 537 prisoners of war engaged on the line in Groups 3 and 5 1729 died, 771 of them Australians. On 20 November the Japanese ordered that memorial services for prisoners who had died be held at all camps of Groups 3 and 5 in Burma and Thailand. Large crosses were erected at the cemeteries and a letter of condolence was read by Colonel Nagatomo to prisoners at the 55 kilometres Camp and by his representatives to prisoners at other camps. The letter read in part:

> We should like to declare the Japanese troops participated in the joys and sorrows of the prisoners of war and native labourers in the construction work and by no means completed, or intended to complete the work only at the sacrifice of the prisoners of war. The Director of Construction cherished the motto 'Prisoners of war and labourers are Fathers of Construction' and constantly endeavoured to improve the treatment of prisoners of war.

The line produced many unsung heroes, one of whom was the commander of 'A' Force, Brigadier Varley, who lost his life in 1944 when the Japanese transport taking him and his work force to Japan was sunk by American submarines off Hainan. Colonel C.G. Anderson, who won the Victoria Cross during the Malayan campaign, paid him this tribute:

> During the whole of this tragic period of misery and suffering Brigadier Varley's strong personality, his vigorous and fearless championship of the troops, careless of rebuffs and determined to leave no stone unturned for the better treatment of the men, won for him the grudging respect of the Japanese and I have no hesitation in saying was probably instrumental in preventing a far greater tragedy than that which took place.

Among the men themselves acts of courage and compassion were daily occurrences and some men lived under the continuous threat of death—for example, Lieutenant Watchorn and Sapper Stephenson of the 2/12th Field Company who operated a radio set in Burma which kept their fellow prisoners informed of the progress of the war in other areas and their optimism at a high level. Throughout the period the dedication, patience and skill of the medical officers was outstanding and without them many fewer men would have survived.

Among the Australians in particular even the darkest day did not quite extinguish the sense of humour which had manifested itself among the diggers of World War I and in other theatres of World War II. One such example was a song written by Gunner ('Major') Conway, of the 2/10th Field Regiment, at the 105 Kilometre Camp in Burma, about his mate who in pre-captivity days had been noted for his gentlemanly reserve and shyness of women. It was sung to the tune of 'The Drover's Dream'.

It happened in the grass, near the Three Pagoda Pass
Where the bamboo bends before the Burma breeze.
Old man moon was riding high, lighting up the tropic sky
When a lovely lady stepped out of the trees.

A melody divine came from lips as red as wine,
As she crooned the jungle changed to paradise.
Enchanted by her song soft I touched her silk sarong
Then she turned to me in maidenly surprise.

Oh soldier boy, she said our love can never be
The heart you seek to win's no longer mine
It was stolen long ago by a bloke I think you know
He was bludging when they built the railway line.

He was big and strong and true and he wore the
  red and blue*
And we welcomed him wherever he appeared
And I still record the shock when he was chock-a-block
And he stroked my titties with his golden beard

So I left her in the grass near the Three Pagoda Pass
Where the bamboo bends before the Burma breeze
In my dreams I see her there with an orchid in her hair
Making love to Jamison neath the jungle trees.

* Artillery colour patch

42 Gunner Richard Gilman, 2/10 Field Regiment, a member of 'A' Force in Burma, was present at the ceremony of the joining of the railway in October 1943. After the war he joined the Department of External Affairs and ironically his first diplomatic posting was to Rangoon, Burma.

43 The first train at Konkoita. On 16 October 1943 the line from Burma joined with the line from Thailand. For a week before this momentous occasion the line-laying parties, reinforced by 300 Dutch prisoners, had laid rails at a frantic pace, at one stage working 33 hours straight. [P406/40/4]

44 The opening ceremony at Konkoita on 25 October 1943. A senior Japanese officer ceremoniously attempted to drive in the last spike while a military band played and film crews went into action. Gunner Richard Gilman of 2/10 Field Regiment, one of the prisoners present, recalls that selected prisoners were issued with new shorts, shirts and footwear for the film. When the filming was completed 'the "film stars" were deprived of their bounty by an unsmiling Japanese quartermaster and his staff who walked down the line of dandified prisoners collecting their uniforms in large bags and leaving the men standing bare in their G-strings'. [P406/40/01]

45 A Japanese film crew photographing prisoners of war at what they described as a bar. Like the temporary issue of shorts for the opening ceremony, this was a propaganda operation. At a few camps along the railway the Japanese provided canteens where seaweed, fruit and a few others items could be purchased. Mostly these facilities were provided only after the completion of the railway. [P406/40/24]

46 Prisoner-of-war graves at Ronsi in Burma. In many of the jungle camps the dead were buried in hasty unmarked graves or cremated in open fires. Australian deaths numbered 479 in Burma and 2336 in Thailand. The total number of prisoner-of-war deaths is estimated at 13 000. [P406/40/31]

47 Japanese engineers paying homage to their dead. Of the 13 000 engineers and guards on the railway some 1000 died. The ratio of deaths was approximately one in every four for prisoners of war, one in every three for Asian labourers and one in every thirteen for the Japanese. [P406/40/23]

Dispersal

8

After the completion of the railway in October 1943 pressure on the prisoners of war eased and conditions improved. In January 1944 the Japanese engineers moved to Burma and were replaced by administrative troops who were of a superior type, but the damage had been done and improved conditions came too late to halt the avalanche of death caused by the monsoon period of the railway's construction. The survivors of 'F' and 'H' Forces were returned to Singapore and most other parties concentrated on relatively comfortable camps at Tamuan, Chungkai, Kanchanaburi, Nakom Pathon and Non Pladuck.

Although there is some evidence that the immensity of the human cost of the railway was beginning to dawn on the Japanese authorities, they proceeded to cull the so-called fit men from the survivors for shipment to Japan to bolster the now hard-hit home industries. Prisoners who remained in Thailand were required to work on maintenance on the line, to build roads and carry out other miscellaneous tasks. Their improved circumstances were somewhat offset by increasing Allied air activity along the line.

The Japan parties were railed either to Singapore or Saigon where they were overloaded onto cargo ships for the hazardous voyage to Japan. All the ships were harassed by prowling American submarines and some were sunk with heavy losses.

I was in one of the first of such parties, assembled at Tamuan camp in Thailand in June 1944, to go to Japan. Like most other men in the group I regarded the possible dangers of a sea voyage as preferable to the prospect of being sent back to the jungle to maintain the railway line. Allied bombers had been flying over our camps since the previous Christmas and we were certain there would soon be heavy demands for labour to repair bombed bridges and other parts of the line. Also the fear of cholera preyed on my mind as it did on others. Accordingly I was relieved to be one of 1000 Australians under the command of Major Reg Newton who boarded a ship in Singapore which sailed for Japan on 4 July 1944.

The voyage lasted 70 days and after leaving Manila our convoy was subjected to constant submarine attacks, most of the tankers being torpedoed before our arrival at the port of Moji in Japan. Two other groups of prisoners of war from Burma and Thailand were less fortunate and their fate was tragic and ironic after surviving the horrors of the railway.

In early September 1944, 2300 prisoners of war under Brigadier Varley embarked in Singapore on the *Kachidoki Maru* and the *Rokyu Maru*. On board the *Rokyu Maru* were 599 British and 649 Australian prisoners of war among whom was Captain C.R.B. Richards of AAMC attached to 2/15 Field Regiment. The prison ships sailed in a convoy on 6 September 1944 while to the north a wolf pack of American submarines known as Ben's Busters lay in wait. The three submarines, *Growler*, *Pampanito* and *Sealion* contacted the convoy by radar some 300 miles off Hainan.

What happened next is recorded in a sworn statement by Captain Richards held in the Australian War Memorial in Canberra:

> At about 0100 hrs, 12 Sep, the convoy was attacked by submarines. One escort, 1 transport or oil tanker were sunk. The convoy continued in formation and was again attacked at about 0500 hrs.
>
> According to estimates made later, 2 destroyers, oil tanker and 2 transports, including the 'Rokyu Maru' were sunk as a result of this attack. The 'Rokyu Maru' was struck by 2 torpedoes, 1 amidships below the waterline and 1 forward on the waterline. Immediately, the ship's Captain, crew and the guards abandoned ship in 9 life boats and 1 smaller boat. No instructions were given to the PW.
>
> The PWs then, according to the pre-arranged plan, threw over the rubber blocks, rafts, hatch covers and other wooden structures.
>
> The sick were assisted off the ship and the majority of the remainder followed. The whole operation was carried out in an orderly fashion and there was no obvious evidence of panic among the PW. . .
>
> During the day 12 Sep, we remained close to the Japanese survivors in the other life boats. Before dusk Japanese destroyers picked up Japanese survivors and we took over their life boats and then went among the rafts and picked up PW survivors. We re-distributed our load into 3 life boats.

On the morning 13 Sep, we saw 8 life boats in line to the north of our 3 boats which had remained together during the night. Later in the day one of them left the others and joined us. In the evening the remaining 7 were seen to go about and sail in an easterly direction while we continued to sail in a westerly direction.

At approx. 0900 hrs, 14 Sep, sounds thought to be gun fire were heard to the north of us. A short while later 3 Japanese destroyers appeared and one of them picked up the PW survivors (80 Australians and British) from the 4 life boats in our vicinity...

When we were taken aboard the destroyer we told one of the Japanese officers that there were a further 7 life boats to the north of us. He indicated that he already knew and pointed to the other destroyers. At the time we believed that the PWs were aboard other destroyers but we later found that this was not so and we concluded that as there were no known survivors those 7 life boats were sunk by the destroyers.

While on the destroyer we received 2 biscuits and approx. two thirds of a pint of water per man during 23 hours.

After picking us up the destroyer sailed in a westerly direction and at approx. 1100 hours, 15 Sep, we were transferred in Hainanto Harbour to an oil tanker where we joined approx. 700 survivors from the *Kachidoki Maru* which was also sunk later in the evening of 12 Sep...

There were 2 other transports and 3 escorts in the convoy and on the way to Moji 2 transports and 2 escorts were sunk.

After our arrival in Japan 1 Australian and 9 British were left at Moji as they were unfit to travel, even by Japanese standards. Five hundred British remained in Tokio and 50 Australians remained in Yokohama while the remaining 261 British and 29 Australians were taken to Sakata. I was with this last party...

After attacking the convoy on 12 September 1944 the American submarines returned to the scene between 13 and 17 September and picked up 141 surviving prisoners including 80 Australians. The rest perished. The patrol report of the submarine *Pampanito* recorded the rescue:

As men were received on board, we stripped them and removed most of the heavy coating of oil and muck. We cleared the after torpedo room and passed them below as quickly as possible. Gave all the men a piece of cloth moistened with water to suck on. All of them were exhausted after four days on the raft and three years' imprisonment. Many had lashed themselves to their makeshift rafts which were slick with grease; and had nothing but life belts with them. All showed signs of pellagra, beri-beri, immersion, salt water sores, ringworm, malaria etc. All were very thin and showed the results of undernourishment. Some were in very bad shape, but with the excitement of rescue they came alongside with cheers for the Yanks and many a curse for the Nips.

It was quite a struggle to keep them on the raft while we took them off one by one. They could not manage to secure a line to the raft, so we sent men over the side who did the job. The survivors came tumbling aboard and then collapsed with strength almost gone. A pitiful sight none of us will ever forget. All hands turned to with a will and the men were cared for as rapidly as possible.

The survivors were taken to Saipan and thence to Australia. There they revealed to Australia and the world for the first time the grim and tragic story of the Burma–Thailand railway. Those prisoners who arrived safely in Japan, by then heavily beleaguered by American air attacks, were dispersed to mines, factories and dockyards and their experiences are a separate story.

After the war ended on 15 August 1945 there was a vast stocktaking of the prisoners of war scattered throughout former Japanese-held territories. The official war history, *The Japanese Thrust*, sums up the Australian experience:

> More than one-third of the Australian soldiers who were prisoners of the Japanese died in captivity: 13 872 were recovered and 7777 died—nearly three times the number killed in battle in, for example, the 9th Australian Division during its four campaigns. Among the 7777 who died, 123 were officers. Of those who did not return from Japanese prison camps, 2336 died in Thailand, 1783 in Borneo, 718 in Ambon, 479 in Burma, 284 in Malaya, 200 in New Britain, 190 in Japan. The number lost at sea was 1515; 27 were executed for attempted escape, 193 were known to have been executed for other reasons and 375 others are believed to have been executed. By comparison of 7116 Australian soldiers who were prisoners of Germany and Italy only 242 died in captivity.

48   A survivor of the Japanese transport *Rokyu Maru* sunk by the submarine USS *Sealion* in heavy seas as the submarine USS *Queenfish* comes alongside for the rescue. He was one of 2300 prisoners of war shipped from Singapore on 6 September 1944 on the *Kachidoki Maru* and the *Rokyu Maru*. Both transports together with eight other Japanese ships in the convoy were sunk by three United States submarines, *Sealion*, *Growler* and *Pampanito*, in an attack which began off Hainan on 12 September 1944. American submarines rescued 159 prisoner-of-war survivors, including 80 Australians, and carried them to freedom. Japanese naval craft picked up another 520 survivors who remained in captivity. [45410]

49   Nakom Pathon prisoner-of-war hospital, Thailand. [P406/40/05]

50 The so-called 'bridge on the River Kwai' after a bombing raid during World War II. It was brought complete from Java to replace the wooden bridge made famous by Pierre Bouille in his book *The Bridge on the River Kwai* and by the film of the same title. There is now no trace of the original wooden bridge which was 300 metres downstream of its existing successor. The bridge is in use today and the trains which travel over it up to Nam Tok on the site of the former prisoner-of-war camp of Tarsau are popular tourist attractions. [122329]

51 A 200-foot bridge built by prisoners of war about ten miles south of Thanbyuzayat after low-level attacks by RAF Liberators on 22 March 1945. In the closing stages of the war such raids caused casualties among prisoners of war held in Thailand and Burma to maintain the railway. At this time also the railway was being used to evacuate sick and wounded Japanese and survivors from their defeat in Burma. [128457]

52 Hideous ulcers caused many amputations on the Burma—Thailand railway. These men are wearing artificial limbs made in Changi by W.O. Arthur Puden of East Maitland, NSW. Left to right: Pte Max Bradford, Moore Park, Sydney, NSW; L/Cpl Jack Campbell, Apollo Bay, Vic.; Pte Steve Gleeson, Mundijong, WA; Pte Alex McKenzie, Boggabri, NSW. [19327]

53 Bangkok, Thailand 15 September 1945. Lieutenant Colonel E.E. Dunlop, commanding officer 2/2 Casualty Clearing Station (right) and Lieutenant Colonel A.E. Coates, chief medical officer, POW hospital at Nakom Paton outside their office at the Medical Headquarters. These two fine surgeons along with their colleagues were responsible for saving the lives of thousands of prisoners of war. The medical officers were the main barriers not only between prisoners and myriad diseases but between overworked slaves and their relentlessly brutal guards. Even today 'Weary' Dunlop is the hero and father figure to survivors of the Burma—Thailand railway. [117362]

54 A latrine at a POW camp designed so that waste matter assists garden cultivation. The condition of the prisoners suggests that the picture may have been taken at the end of hostilities. [157869]

55 Bangkok, Thailand, 14 September 1945. Captain R.H.C. Stubb, 4 Anti-Tank Regiment, left, and Major R.H. Barraclough, 2/10 Field Regiment, studying a wall chart showing POW camps at the POW Branch HQ, Recovered Allied POW and Internees Unit. [117347]

56 A prisoner-of-war rice-carrying party at Saraburi, Thailand. The general condition of the prisoners and the fact that the photograph has been taken quite openly suggests that the picture may have been taken at the conclusion of hostilities. By this time food supplies were plentiful although most of the men were barefooted and reduced to wearing lap-laps. [157880]

Return to the River Kwai

9

In 1978, 35 years after the completion of the Burma–Thailand railway I went back, this time in comfort with my wife. Whereas my first journey to Thailand from Singapore had taken five days enclosed with 35 other Australians in a steel rice carriage, this journey, in a Thai Airlines DC 10, took three and a half hours. From Bangkok we travelled in an air-conditioned minibus for a further three hours to an area on the River Kwai, 70 kilometres upstream from Kanchanaburi (Kanburi) where some of the worst wartime atrocities had occurred.

We disembarked at the River Kwai Village, a luxury complex of 60 air-conditioned units built by a Thai family company three years previously. Overlooking the muddy waters of the Kwai River, the holiday complex has a spacious dining room and bar and at the end of the surrounding tropical garden is a swimming pool fed by a waterfall which tumbles from an overhanging cliff. We studied a map and talked to our Thai hosts who told us we were only one kilometre upstream from the former POW camp of Tonchan and that within 20 kilometres upstream had been the camps of Konyu and Hintok, in both of which I had once served time.

The next morning a Thai guide led us along a jungle path to all that remained of Tonchan camp—two crumbling concrete ovens from the former Japanese cookhouse beside a spring. The spring was still feeding a rivulet which ended in a waterfall over a cliff into the river. Tonchan once housed a POW officers' working party. This was the party of officers, 320-strong, including 68 Australians, sent there from Changi in May 1943. They had been told that they would be employed on camp administration and supervision duties. When they arrived, however, they were put to work clearing jungle, felling trees, carting logs and other work more suitable for beasts of burden. Although 30 per cent of them were physically unfit and the majority were older men excluded from previous work forces, they were almost daily encouraged to greater effort with pick handles and iron bars. By June 1943 half of the party was incapacitated, mainly from tropical ulcers.

We retreated from this gloomy place and met another Thai guide who had promised to take us upriver in his fast longboat, which resembled a surf ski, a little wider and about six times as long. It was powered, not by an outboard motor, but by a big truck engine mounted on a swivel aft. A propellor was attached to its long tail shaft. Leaving behind a continuous explosion of spray and a wake like a furrow in a ploughed field, we sped up the river, negotiating bends within inches of protruding rocks and trees and sometimes skimming through reeds by the river bank. Coming to the area between Konyu and Hintok I observed that the river was as beautiful as I had sometimes remembered. There was little else of beauty to remember. Signs of habitation along the banks and occasional clearings revealed huts and plantations that were postwar developments.

I wondered whether this could be the same place where more than a generation ago a wretched army of slaves had laboured so hopelessly; where cholera had moved stealthily through a watery world, leaving behind so many scanty graves and hasty funeral pyres. It was the same place, but from the river nothing was visible to confirm it. A little over four kilometres up that range on the eastern side of the river was the site of Konyu camp and near it the cutting on which I had started work on Anzac Day 1943. Hintok camp was a few kilometres further up the river but nothing remained of it.

On the way back to the River Kwai village our guide promised to take us downriver on the following day, beyond where the railway now ended, to the station of Lok Sum where we would board the train and travel to its present terminus at Nam Tok, alias the former POW base and hospital camp of Tarsau. Nam Tok is 77 kilometres upstream from Kanchanaburi.

The journey downstream was even more terrifying than the one the previous day because the river was running fast from monsoon rains. There were signs of life everywhere. Small farmlets carved into the riverside jungle, timber loading ramps, people bathing, and barges towing rafts of bamboo. I recognised the site of Tarsau camp, at which were moored about 100 river boats. Beside them a river petrol station was busy servicing river craft. Beyond this little settlement was the terminal station of the railway, Nam Tok. I vividly remembered Nam Tok when it was Tarsau. Returning to it by barge at the end of July 1943 had been like entering the gates of paradise. Then it was a huge primitive hospital base daily receiving barge loads of human wrecks evacuated from upriver jungle camps. Most of the men who completed the journey were emaciated skeletons, others did not survive the journey.

Skimming further downstream another familiar relic of the past came into view—the site of Wampo, the scene of my first tough job on the railway. There we worked on a huge embankment and although only engaged for a little over a fortnight we left behind 120 men. The railway line had been laid along a rickety viaduct approaching the embankment and we were holding up progress. I remembered an all-out effort which involved a shift of 30 hours straight. At the end of it dozens of unconscious men were carried back to camp. Beyond Wampo was the viaduct, triple-tiered and 200 metres long. Much of the original woodwork remains but some reconstruction is evident. As we studied this seemingly dangerous structure a modern train suddenly rounded a bend and crawled along the cliff face. We reached the river landing of Lok Sum after one and a half hours and walked inland to the railway station, just in time to buy tickets and board the train.

The journey from Lok Sum, via Wang Poh (Wampo) back to Nam Tok (Tarsau) took one hour and, apart from the perilous viaduct stretch, the journey was very much like a ride on the Canberra–Sydney train. We passed through about six stations along the way, indicating a reasonably substantial population and some development in the area. Nam Tok was a big surprise. What I remembered as a collection of long attap huts full of malaria, dysentery and ulcer-ridden skeletons was now a town complete with shops, streets and houses.

The 'death railway' as the Thais call it, is bound in time to outlive its name and this whole chapter in our history will remain only as one of the facets of Thailand's fast-growing tourist industry. What will remain is the cemetery at Kanchanaburi where lie the remains of 6982 Allied prisoners of war, 1362 of them Australians. Two miles away across the river at Chung Kai is another cemetery with an additional 1740 graves. I walked among the headstones at Kanchanaburi looking for the names of men of my unit, the 2/10 Field Regiment, and each name conjured up a face and a personality I had long forgotten. It was like taking part in a ghostly roll-call and for a moment I wished I had never returned.

A few kilometres from the cemetery is the so-called bridge on the River Kwai, a large steel-span structure on concrete pylons. It is not, however, the original bridge about which the book was written or the subject of the film (made in Ceylon). No trace remains of the original wooden bridge built by prisoners of war some 300 metres downstream from the steel-and-concrete structure. The existing bridge was brought complete from Java during the war.

Back at Nam Tok where the railway now ends I walked north along the still

83

well-defined bed of the track. My guide told me that the rails had been pulled up years ago but that at one stage the Thai government had considered restoring the line through to Burma. This idea had been abandoned after a government minister inspecting the track was accidentally killed by a fall of rock in one of the cuttings. In any case, he added, a good motor highway is being built. Such was the end of this gigantic engineering achievement built at incalculable cost which Britain in October 1946 agreed to sell to the Thai government for the bargain price of £1.5 million.

57 The author and his wife Patricia with Pradivick Mahapunyo, a Buddhist monk who looks after the railway museum at Kanchanaburi. The main museum building is a replica of a typical POW hut and contains an interesting collection of paintings, sketches and relics illustrating facets of POW life. [photo taken August 1978]

58 The bridge on the River Kwai in 1978. It is widely publicised by tourist organisations and is much used by trains, pedestrians and light traffic. [Photo H.V. Clarke]

59 A passenger train carrying tourists and local residents across the viaduct at Wampo in July 1978. There was no local habitation in the area in 1943 and the concrete buttresses supporting the bridge were postwar additions. Banana and other plantations are now installed in what was virgin jungle before the war. [Photo H.V. Clarke]

60 Lok Sum railway station on what is left of the Burma–Thailand railway. There were no intermediate stations on the wartime railway. [photo H.V. Clarke]

61 The town of Nam Tok, formerly Tarsau prisoner-of-war camp, is 77 kilometres beyond the bridge on the River Kwai at Kanchanaburi. Tarsau was a vast hospital camp towards the end of 1943 and into it poured the survivors of horror camps further north. There the barges unloaded the dead and dying as well as those lucky enough to survive. Here in July 1978 the author and his wife were astonished to see a pink poodle in one of the shops. [Photo H.V. Clarke]

62 A typical station on the railway between Lok Sum and Nam Tok—the former prisoner-of-war camp of Tarsau. Until after the war there were no railway stations between Kanchanaburi in Thailand and Thanbyuzayat, only rough sidings at various camps along the line. Civilisation has come to the River Kwai. [Photo H.V. Clarke]

63 The luxury River Kwai tourist village photographed in 1978 from the site of the former Tonchan prisoner-of-war camp. All that remained of the camp were a few old stone foundations of the old Japanese kitchens. The River Kwai was at a low level and the long boat coming downstream is the fastest form of transport on the river today. [Photo H.V. Clarke]

64 A long boat on the River Kwai and its relaxed pilot-driver. The long boat is powered by a big truck engine. Such craft can reach high speeds and are in use in the canals of Bangkok as well as on the rivers. They ride low in the water and passengers are often drenched with spray. [Photo H.V. Clarke]

65 Nam Tok, the last station on the existing railway line from Kanchanaburi in Thailand. Tourists are transported from here to a luxury tourist motel further north on the River Kwai. Few signs of the barbaric prisoner-of-war times are evident.
[Photo H.V. Clarke]

66 Kanchanaburi war cemetery where lie the remains of 6982 prisoners of war, 1362 of them Australians.
[Photo H.V. Clarke]

67 The end of the line in 1978. Further north only the bed of the line remains.
[Photo H.V. Clarke]

68   The largest, oldest and highest Buddhist pagoda in Thailand is the Phra Pathon Chedi at Nakom Pathon, 56 kilometres from Bangkok. Buddhism was first introduced to the Thai people at Nakom Pathon, which was the country's capital from the tenth to the fifteenth century. The enormous golden tiled dome of the pagoda rears 380 feet towards the sky and can be seen for miles. It was a famous landmark to thousands of Australian prisoners of war on their way to and from the Burma–Thailand railway during World War II. After the railway was completed the Japanese became concerned by the massive cost in human life and established a number of greatly improved camps and hospitals to house the survivors. One such hospital built as Nakom Pathon and under the command of Lieutenant Colonel A.E. Coates held 8000 prisoners of war. [Photo H.V. Clarke]

69   Corporal J.G. (Tom) Morris, 22 Brigade HQ, was a member of 'A' Force in Burma and was still working on the railway when the war ended. Now a retired headmaster in Canberra, he initiated the move to have Hell Fire Pass restored as a memorial to prisoners of war who died on the Burma – Thailand railway and to Thais who helped prisoners with medicine and food.

70   Tom Morris in Canberra 1984.

71 Mr Jim Appleby, Snowy Mountains Engineering Corporation engineer in Hell Fire Pass, Thailand, 3 February 1985. Hell Fire Pass was the scene of a last desperate rush by the Japanese to complete their supply line on schedule. Some 1000 prisoners of war worked day and night cutting through solid rock. Four hundred died in the completion of the 600-metre Hell Fire section alone and by mid-August 1943 there were 100 survivors only.

72 Tourists on the bridge over the River Kwai, Kanchanaburi, 1 January 1985

73 Old rails near Nam Tok station, formerly Tarsau POW camp. Jim Appleby checked the markings which indicated that they were original rails taken from Malaya to build the Burma–Thailand railway. He suggested that some could be laid in Hell Fire Pass for display.

Hell Fire Pass memorial, Thailand

10

Since 1978 the number of former prisoners of war returning to Thailand has increased yearly. Former Corporal J.G. (Tom) Morris of 22 Brigade HQ, now a retired Canberra headmaster, returned twice to the Burma–Thailand railway, in 1983 and 1984. His visits provoked the following recollections and surprising consequences which he records:

On 24th December 1943, the second last group of 253 patients from the 55 k. 'hospital' entrained for the slow and exhausting 310 k. journey to Tamarkan POW camp, Thailand. We were accommodated in steel vans, normally used for the transport of rice, 28 per van or 8 stretcher cases, plus two seated on the floor, and 2 medical orderlies. With a minimum issue of meals, and the complete absence of drinking water, beyond what we carried in our water bottles, the journey was somewhat uncomfortable to say the least. The ray of hope that kept us going was the expectation of better conditions and medical treatment in our new camp, plus the fact that we were at last leaving that accursed railway behind us.

As we travelled through Thailand, the massive cuttings through solid rock, and the high trestle bridges over ravines and rivers, brought home to us the enormous difficulties which the work-force on this section of the railway had faced during those dreadful 'speedo' months throughout the monsoonal season of 1943. The construction of our Burma cuttings, when compared with those in Thailand, paled into insignificance.

The last few months of the war saw me once again at work on that railway, which I had come to detest and fear so much. Our return to normality began on 20th August 1945, when we boarded a train at Kuei for our journey to Tamuang, where all recovered POW from the area were being concentrated. During the late afternoon of that day, we crawled over a long wooden viaduct, listening somewhat apprehensively as it creaked and groaned under the weight of the train and its passengers. A hundred yards further on, we entered a cutting so narrow that we could almost reach out and touch the solid rock walls which towered above us.

This, I learned later, was the awesome 'Hellfire Pass' complex at Konyu. It was in two sections, one approximately 500 yards long and in places 25 feet deep, and the second, 80 yards long and 80 feet deep. They had been excavated using the most primitive equipment—picks, shovels, chunkels, cane baskets, rice bags, 8 lb hammers, tap drills, a minimum of explosives and, occasionally, a compressor and an elephant or two. The daily quota commenced at 1.5 cubic metres per man per day, but within two days it had been raised to 2 cubic metres, and by the end of the first week to 3 cubic metres.

The men worked in three shifts, and at night the cuttings were lit by a dozen or so carbide lamps, bamboo containers filled with dieseline and rice sacking for wicks, and bamboo fires. Begun on 25th April 1943, the harsh demands of the Japanese, starvation rations, inadequate medical supplies, compounded by an outbreak of cholera, along with malaria, dysentery and tropical ulcers, all took a heavy toll of the POW work-force. Only those unfortunate enough to have worked on 'Hellfire Pass' could ever adequately describe the excruciating months spent on its construction.

Almost forty years later, I was able to gain some small idea of the enormity of this awesome task. In April 1983, I met two people who were to influence me in a decision to endeavour to locate the site of the Konyu cuttings. The first was Alf Comley, 4th Anti-Tank, who as a member of 'D' Force had toiled in their construction, and whom I met when on the 1983 Bamboo Tour. The second was Jim Appleby, Senior Resident Engineer at the Khao Laem Dam project, which is situated in the area of the old Takanun railway camps. Jim proved to be quite knowledgeable about the old railway trace, much of which has now disappeared—some to the modern requirements of farm produce; some in its reversion to the bamboo and jungle it was before our encroachment in 1943. He had a keen desire to find 'Hellfire Pass', but the pressure of work had so far precluded him from achieving his aim.

On my return to Canberra, I began a search of War Memorial documents to find out more about Konyu. As I read, there built up within me a sense of urgency of purpose—to locate 'Hellfire Pass' myself. With this aim, and the blessing of my wife, my brother Eric and I set off on that pilgrimage in February 1984. Earlier, I had written to the Kanchanaburi branch of the Tourism Authority of Thailand, seeking assistance in the provision of a suitable guide and vehicle. The help and friendship of Mr Pairoat Prokkaew, from the Tourism Authority, was to prove to be the lynch pin of our success.

On 8th February, armed with letters of introduction, we caught the train from Kanchanaburi to Nam Tok, where we were met by our guide and taken to the River Kwai Hotel, which is situated near the old Tonchan area. Later that afternoon we set off on our self-imposed task. Perhaps my diary, written that evening, best describes the occasion:

> Having located the Governmental Experimental Cattle Farm, our guide presented our letter of introduction, and was given permission to escort us through the farm to the old railway site. Here, the ballast was scattered about, and it was difficult to recognise the embankment area. As we moved on, it became more clearly defined, with large pieces of ballast still in position. We shortly approached what was the first section of this complex. It was more like a shelf gouged out of the side of the mountain slope, rather than a cutting, with the scars of drill and blasting still clearly evident on its side.
>
> A little further on we crossed the remains of what had been a short viaduct across a small stream. The timber work has rotted away, but the stone abutting the banks of the stream are still just as they were placed forty years ago. A short distance on was a sight I shall never forget. There stood the cutting through which I had passed on that August afternoon many years ago. My God, what a daunting sight it must have been for those poor POW when they saw just what was expected of them on that April day of 1943!
>
> Entering the cutting, now lined with small saplings reaching upwards for the sunlight denied to them by the surrounding jungle, I found myself filled with emotion—sorrow, reverence, awe, and

above all, a sense of privilege that I was at last able to stand in this almost sacred place.

As we made our way through Hellfire Pass, over ballast and rotting sleepers, I was struck by the absolute silence. Not even the sound of a bird disturbed the peace of our surroundings. What a contrast this would have been to the noise of hammers, compressors and explosives; the rantings and ravings of sadistic Japanese engineers and Korean guards, as these human ants attacked this mammoth task. Names like Itchnoi, Battlegong, Mussolini, Hazama and The Maggot, about whom I had read and heard so much, came surging forth, and I experienced a feeling of deep hatred and revulsion for the Japanese and their Korean counterparts.

Moving through the northern exit, we came to the end of the embankment in this section. The next 50 yards was the site of a long wooden viaduct which had once spanned a wide ravine. No timber work remains, but the stone abutments at each end of the site are still in perfect condition. In the ravine itself lie undisturbed the hundreds of tons of rock which had been removed from the cutting and dumped into position to help shore up the foundations of the weird wooden trestle bridge that once crossed it.

Beyond this point, the bamboo and jungle have reclaimed the old railway trace, and I had to turn back. As I was making my way up the stone foundation, I felt something hard under my foot. Raking away the soil in a small niche, I uncovered three 12 inch bridge spikes and eight dog-spikes. Of the latter, five were in mint condition. Clearly stamped into the head of each, were the letters F.M.S.R., 1940. The Japanese had torn up sections of secondary railway in the Federated Malay States, and taken them to Thailand for use in the construction of their railway. That find, together with the photographs I had been able to take, was the climax of our trip.

The following morning, I arranged to revisit the cuttings, as I wanted to take additional photographs, using a second camera. This time I went on alone. While retracing my steps from the northern extremity of the old viaduct site, I decided to follow along the slope of the rockfill. In doing so, I found myself too far down the slope and, on looking up, saw that I had a climb of almost forty feet to reach the top.

As I struggled and clawed my way up, grasping at small saplings and bamboo for leverage, slipping and cutting my hands and legs on the sharp rocks, gasping for breath as I paused and cursed my foolishness, I gained some inkling of what it might have been like for those weak and emaciated POW. Not for them the luxury of a pause, as they repeatedly performed this task, hounded by screaming guards and engineers, and spurred on by blows from bamboo, rifle butts, and rocks thrown at them to ensure their rapid progress. Once was more than enough for me!

Over the next few days, as we made our way to other sections of the railway—Kinsaiyok, Hindato, Takanun—the germ of an idea began to take root. Would it be possible to have Hellfire Pass preserved as an historic site, dedicated to the memory of all our fellow POW and civilian slaves, of whom so much had been demanded in the construction of the Burma—Thailand railway?

At Kanchanaburi, I discussed this possibility with Mr Pairoat Prokkaew, who assured me of the Tourism Authority's support. Upon my return to Canberra, I sought, and readily received, the support of my local member of Parliament, Mr Ken Fry.

The result was action by Mr Barry Cohen, then Minister for Home Affairs and Environment, in June 1984 to begin negotiations between Australia and the Thailand authorities to conserve and maintain the Konyu cuttings. This involved the co-operation of the Department of Foreign Affairs and the Snowy Mountains Engineering Corporation. Coordination of the project is being undertaken by the Australian—Thai Chamber of Commerce.

On 22 July 1985 Mr Barry Cohen, Minister for Arts, Heritage and Environment, announced an Australian Government grant of $25 000 for the preservation of a section of the Burma—Thailand railway as a memorial to those Australian and British prisoners of war who died during its construction in World War II. It has been proposed that the memorial be dedicated also to those Thais who risked their lives supplying medicine and food to prisoners of war who built the railway during those dangerous times.

Meanwhile in Thailand, Mr Jim Appleby, senior resident engineer at Khao Laem Dam project, has àlready carried out a preliminary reconnaissance of the Hell Fire Pass area and the following photographs taken by him show that part of the railway as it exists today.

74 Disused footbridge built from railway materials in the position of an original railway bridge, 62 kilometres from Kanchanaburi and 400 metres from the popular tourist spot, Sai Yok waterfall.

75 Footbridge pillars built from railway sleepers.

76 Sai Yok waterfall, 27 February 1985. The person standing directly in front of the fall is standing on the Burma–Thailand railway.

77 Wat Phu Takiang, a photograph taken from edge of highway 120 kilometres from Kanchanaburi and 10 kilometres on the Bangkok side of Hell Fire Pass.

78 Wat Phu Takiang. The two small buildings at the back sit on a railway embankment. Sleeper depressions in front of the buildings have been filled with concrete, which makes a permanent record of where they were.

79 Wat Phu Takiang. Steps to an embankment on the Burma–Thailand railway.

80   A stone
embankment of the
railway behind Wat
Phu Takiang.

81 A train at Nam Tok railway station, 3 February 1985.

82 Entrance to Thai Army beef cattle station on which Hell Fire Pass is located.

83 A railway sleeper which had been pulled out of the ground. Access to Hell Fire Pass is along the railway.

84 Old railway sleepers on the approach to Hell Fire Pass.

85 The railway at Nam Tok looking towards Bangkok. Old sleepers are piled in the foreground.

86 Khun Somkiran points to a drill hole in the rock wall of Hell Fire Pass, 3 February 1985. After over 40 years such marks of the terrible labour forced on prisoners of war are as stark as when first created.

87 Snowy Mountains Engineering Corporation engineer Jim Appleby in the bed of Hell Fire Pass, February 1985. Plans are in hand to clear the timber and re-lay the sleepers and rails as a memorial to the prisoners of war who died during construction of the railway.